On-Demand Learning:
Training in the New Millennium

By Darin E. Hartley, M.Ed.

With an Introduction by John Coné
Vice President of Dell Learning

HRD Press
Amherst, Massachusetts

Published by: 4/03

HRD Press
22 Amherst Road
Amherst, MA 01002
1-800-822-2801 (U.S. and Canada)
413-253-3488
413-253-3490 (FAX)
www.hrdpress.com

ISBN 0-87425-539-2

Cover design by Donna Thibault-Wong
Editorial services by Robie Grant
Production services by Clark T. Riley

Table of Contents

Acknowledgments

There are many people who helped me with this forward-looking work. I must thank my wife for continued encouragement and ongoing support. I must also thank Chris Hunter of HRD Press for working with me in the development of the proposal for this book and for his ready acceptance of the idea behind the book. I thank all of the support staff at HRD Press, who have helped edit, publish, and market the book in a variety of ways. In particular, Brian Houle has been invaluable to me in the pursuit of alternative marketing strategies and I appreciate his dedication and insights.

I must share thanks with the many people at Dell Computer Corporation who continue to be a source of inspiration, innovation, leadership, and friendship. I'd like to express great gratitude and appreciation to John Coné, the Vice President of Dell Learning, for providing the insightful Introduction to this book and again for continuing to push me to find the best solution to business problems. Thank you David Jedrziewski and David Finkel (for editorial reads and great input), Jefferson Raley, and the team I manage at Dell for the continuous learning opportunities offered to me. I'd also like to thank our many internal clients who believe in what we do and help us provide a learning edge for their constituents.

Stephanie Powell worked with me from initial design in implementation of learn2now.com. She humbly downplays her contribution, but it has been a tremendous one. I hope to work with her on other projects in the future.

I'd also like to thank those people who bought my first book, *Job Analysis at the Speed of Reality*, and for the useful commentary and positive feedback they have provided. I express my gratitude to those people who used the book as a tool to conduct their own streamlined job analysis sessions.

Finally, and probably most importantly, I thank the countless people out there who have shared ideas, best practices, and examples of on-demand learning for me... and now for all of you. These collaborators include Janice Bahary, Maurice Rondeau, Darcy Kurtz, Clay Curtis, Trudy Lonegan, Susan Hanley, Linda Jacard, Scott Boston, David Johnson, Kristin Nelson, Larry Golden, Beth Thomas, Dan Bryant, and Laurie Gordon. If I have not given someone credit here, I apologize, but please realize that any missed acknowledgments were accidental and not malicious.

Fast Foreword

Look around you. I'll bet that right now, somewhere within your reach or within a couple of feet of you, is something that enables you to complete a task easier and faster. There's something that makes your life easier or empowers you to do things that would normally be unthinkable.

Are you in your den or family room reading this? Then you probably have a remote control for your television, another one for your sound system, light switches, dimmers, heating and/or cooling system control, and so forth. Are you at work in your office or cubicle? You probably have a powerful personal computer on your desk with access to the Internet, multiline phone with voice mail, fax machine, printers, a personal digital assistant, and/or many other self-service tools. Are you on an airplane flying at 33,000 feet? You may have a portable computer, access to an in-flight phone, in-flight movies, or video games. Technology-enabled tools, useful gadgets, and disposable items surround us, entertain us, provide us services, and make our lives easier. Society is expecting more and more of these things all of the time. The expectations created by self-service tools are crossing over into the realms of education and learning.

The next millennium will be the beginning of a learning revolution unlike anything witnessed in many years. Learners want to be able to learn things when they want to learn things, whether it is at 3 a.m. or at 10:00 p.m. Learners want to learn in their homes, in their cars, in their cubicles at work, on the manufacturing floor, and while they are away from their home offices. And when possible, learners want to get the learning just before they have the need for it. This means people are going to be less than happy about sitting through three days of training on Microsoft Excel™ (a powerful spreadsheet application) to learn how to insert a formula into a cell. How do we get these users the information and/or knowledge they need without forcing them to get disproportionate amounts of training on extraneous aspects of the application? How do we make learning for people as accessible and easy as many of the everyday tools that we use? And finally, how do we provide learning opportunities for people in such a fashion that they oftentimes will not even know they are learning? My favorite example of this is the Automatic Teller Machine (ATM) at the bank. You can get money around the world, twenty-four hours day, from literally thousands of machines. Each time you use one, you are being trained to use it … even though you've probably never equated it with training in the past. The same is true of debit machines at supermarkets and other retail sites. Unintentional learning is often more powerful than intentional learning.

The focus of this book is on providing managers, Human Resource specialists, and training personnel with a forewarning of the impending learning revolution they will experience and ideas to help develop new learning tools to meet the demand for self-service learning. The prevalent on-demand services that are available in other walks of life must be adapted to the education and learning field. Just as traditional brokerage houses are scrambling to react to the groundswell of online brokerages that provide individual investors the power to buy and sell stocks from their living rooms, learning facilitators must be ready to provide similar levels of on-demand learning. Would you rather be like one of the companies that has tapped into empowerment as an essential part of their business model or play catch up like those companies not anticipating the inevitable changes on the way? Merrill Lynch spent $850 million and five years to upgrade their knowledge-based tools for their employees (Gates, p. 82). In order to be more competitive in the finance arena, Merrill Lynch decided to invest in tools designed to empower their workforce into the future.

I hope that after reading this book you will look for ways to provide autonomous learning opportunities for clients, peers, and subordinates. Providing on-demand learning solutions is not something that has to occur all at once. Unleash a couple of these solutions at a time. Learn from your customer base and try to improve each subsequent solution release. It may seem difficult or strange to offer solutions like this, but I promise you, it will be rewarding and empowering not only for you but also for the groups you serve!

I have one other note for readers. On some pages throughout the book you will find little boxes containing nuggets for you to consider. I've called these *Learning Bytes*. They are meant to provoke your thoughts as you read the book. These are summarized on pages 167 and 168 in case you'd like to read them in one location.

Introduction by John Coné

John Coné is one of the most insightful, inspirational personalities I've had the pleasure of ever knowing or working with in my career. He is recognized in the learning and training industry as a leading edge thinker and is sought after by a variety of organizations to consult and/or make presentations. He is currently the Vice President of Dell Learning at Dell Computer Corporation in Austin, Texas. He has run learning organizations for Sequent and Motorola. John is currently on the board of the American Society for Training and Development (ASTD). He is also one of the most skilled people I know at creating a learning metaphor from an ordinary event.

Not long ago I pulled some ligaments in my knee. For the next couple of weeks I found myself cursing my bad luck. Not because I had hurt my knee; but because it seemed that I had managed to hurt it just when I needed to use it the most. Then I remembered the time I sprained my shoulder – just when I had all those things to do that required me to use it. And the time I broke a wrist, only to discover that I had a ton of things to do that week that depended almost exclusively on that wrist. A couple of examples later, I figured it out. There was nothing at all unusual about what I did after hurting my knee, my shoulder, or my wrist. It's just that the strain made me notice myself using them.

I suspect this syndrome applies to lifelong learning. For at least a decade we've talked about lifelong learning as if it is a new phenomenon; as if we'd uncovered a new requirement for success just when we needed to use it. Did we really believe that for centuries people had successful and fulfilling lives and careers without learning a thing after age 21? More likely, it was the strain. As it became harder to keep learning fast enough, we started to hurt. So we noticed ourselves doing something we had been doing all along.

Our responses to the strain were predictable. Just as with an injury, we first tried to do the same things we'd always done the way we'd always done them. If it hurt too much, we accommodated by trying to do the same things we'd always done, but a little (or maybe even a lot) differently. On reflection, it seems to me that the majority of the things we've heralded as advances in corporate education fit into that second category. But what is needed is to *do different things.*

As I thought about my experience with my life's minor medical nuisances, it was easy to draw more parallels with the way organizations react to the inevitable changes in how we must learn as we work. I thought about my doctor's advice regarding a strained Achilles tendon. She first said: "Lay off it for a while." I was to just stop using that muscle. (OK, tendon.) For an addicted runner, the advice was useless. I couldn't just stop. Nor can any of us. In our work lives we run to keep up and we run faster to get ahead. Success isn't about where we are or what we know. It's about where we can be next; what we can learn next, and how soon we can put it to work.

My doctor's next advice was a regimen of icing and stretching, two things I must admit had never been a part of my routine. It seemed to work. In fact, it brought results so quickly that I stopped doing it after about a week. If the pain goes away, how quickly we revert to old habits! But new circumstances, new requirements, are seldom so transient. There was no quick fix, and the pain returned. I paid a price for failing to stick with my new requirements for success.

And that was another lesson to me. New things seldom seem natural. The process of my morning run now took more time, more effort, even more planning. What a nuisance! New things we decide to do are an adventure. New things that we are forced to do are a pain. And yet, over time, the icing and the stretching became a habit. Eventually, I didn't even notice doing them. *So things that were simple before take more planning until they become new habits.*

To my mind, *habit* is a key concept. Often I hear the change agents in our profession talk about "changing the culture," or about "introducing an entirely new system." Another very popular approach is to "get top management to champion the change." Now, all of these are very good concepts, and there are times when one or more are essential. But it seems to me that they also have the potential to overcomplicate the simple change in habit we seek.

I wonder what my reaction would have been had my doctor told me that the key to overcoming my injury was to totally rethink the role of running in my life. "First, we need to get your wife to champion this change in your approach to exercise. She must support — in fact coach —

your stretching and icing. And, after all, running is really just one part of an overall approach to health. That's why you need to change your diet, begin taking these new supplements three times a day, and add anaerobic elements to your exercise routine. And let's talk about removing stress factors in your life...."

If my doctor had taken that approach, I'm sure I could not have denied the value of every bit of the planned program. I am equally sure I would have failed to implement it. For one thing, it proposed to solve a much larger problem than the one causing me pain. For another, it required simultaneous changes across a wide range of very comfortable habits.

I can't tell you how many times I've encountered consultants and gurus who proudly proclaim that they don't even take on a problem unless they get commitment from the top for broad and (complex) systemic change. I stand in respectful awe of the folks who can do that. For me, it's enough to work as simply as possible to help change a single habit. At my best, I can occasionally make such a change seem minor, even transparent. And I've discovered that this incremental approach can work more swiftly than revolutionary macro changes.

And that led to one more metaphorical thought: Doing new things has consequences. I must admit that I skipped the Austin marathon this year due to those torn knee ligaments. I just wasn't confident that I had recovered fully and that my new routine would get me through. The risk wasn't that I would lose the race (I never get close!) or that I would fail to finish. The risk was that I would aggravate the injury so severely that I wouldn't be able to run or walk at all. There's an element of risk in every change, even the unavoidable ones. We need to think about the failure consequences of the changes that we propose to make. Most times, failure to successfully change does not mean a return to the status quo. Things tend to get better, or get worse. We have to consider those risks and find ways to be bold and stay committed to change in the face of them.

This book is about doing different things when it comes to learning in the workplace. There are some great ideas here; actions you can take today to take some of the strain out of lifelong learning in your company. You should steal them.

When you do, you shouldn't expect them all to feel natural at first. Some will, some won't. You should be prepared to take the time to develop new habits and not to revert too quickly if the pain lets up a little. That you are preparing to read this book says you already know you don't have a choice. You have to do different things.

But Darin's book is about more than new practices. The most powerful and least obvious aspect of what you'll read here is the underlying philosophy. I say least obvious, because you'll find yourself reacting to much of it with *"OK"* or even *"of course,"* without stopping to think about what it would take to really act on that philosophy. That part of the book is about new ways of thinking about learning, new ways of planning for learning, and new ways of enabling learning.

So learn about the practices. Use them. Improve on them. But don't forget to look behind them to the ideas on which they are based.

Learning Byte *The American Sign Language (ASL) sign for learning is to place the dominant hand into the open, upturned palm of the other hand and quickly pull it up onto the forehead.*

The On-Demand Society

People in the 21st century are spoiled. Spoiled beyond belief, spoiled beyond the wildest dreams of people who lived 100 or even 200 years ago. We can do things every single day whenever we like that would have been considered magic not so long ago. The average person does things on an average day that all the kings' horses and all the kings' men couldn't do. Yes indeed. We are spoiled and getting more spoiled each minute. Take the simple act of getting to work in the morning.

The millennium man or woman arises at precisely 6:05 a.m. (or 7:19 a.m., or 10:30 a.m.) with a digital alarm clock. He or she can be awakened with an electronic buzzer, a favorite radio station, a CD, or even the recorded sounds of birds, the ocean, or a rainforest. Coffee is already brewing in the electronically programmed coffeepot. A quick flick of the remote control tunes the cable-ready television to CNBC™ so that the weary person can start gathering information about United States and global stock markets. He or she showers in water that can be regulated to just the perfect temperature, and gets dried off in a climate-controlled bathroom. He or she pops a bagel into the toaster which toasts it to just the right shade of brown. After getting dressed and watching some more television, the person logs onto the computer and connects to the Internet. Millennium man or woman checks his or her email, reads his or her horoscope on a web site that has been prefigured *just* for him or her, and logs onto his or her online trading company. Millennium man or woman then places some limit orders to buy shares of XYZ Company and sells some of his shares of the ABC Company. He or she then leaves the house, gets in his or her car, stops at an Automatic Teller Machine (ATM) on the way to work for lunch money. Finally, he or she calls his administrative assistant from the car cellular phone to get some copies made for his or her first meeting of the day. This all happens before 8:00 a.m.

The technology and services rendered to this individual weren't available even to the most powerful leaders of most of recorded time. Yet we daily take them for granted. As our affinity for technology and on-demand service and satisfaction grows, this culture will permeate itself in other parts of life. In particular, the learner will demand equal capability for his or her personal and professional development. Those of us in the training and development arena who are aware of this can take action now to provide learners with what they will soon want regularly. That is, we will need to develop on-demand learning solutions in a variety of media to facilitate learning in the digital age.

What are some other examples of burgeoning technology and the on-demand civilization we are all a part of now? People can routinely send faxes and emails to people around the world from even the most remote locations on our planet (deep within the rainforests in South America and on top of Mount Everest). Communication occurs at a global level with a minimum amount of effort. This is in stark contrast with communication even 100 years ago.

The personal computer is pervasive and nearly a necessity in the home today. We use it to balance our checkbooks, check email, surf the Internet, and play games. We write letters, build financial spreadsheets, send faxes, create graphics, write books, do homework, and trade stock. We check the weather, buy and sell things, conduct research, write business proposals, and figure out our annual federal and state tax returns. We can also learn sign language, take a guitar lesson, listen to music, and so forth, ad infinitum. Everyday we figure out more and more ways to use these tools. The power of the machines on people's desktops is exponentially greater than that of the first computers built; they're also much, much smaller. The first computers were as big as garages and weighed tons. And portable personal computers are immensely more powerful.

People can now buy and sell things twenty-four hours a day from the comfort of their living rooms and home offices. People shop on the Internet, through the television (with networks like QVC™), and with slick catalogs for everything from cigars to lingerie to designer clothing. Amazon.com™ has revolutionized browsing for books, with a tremendous online catalog, discounted prices, and Priority Mail shipment. People are buying large-ticket items as well. As of late 1999, Dell Computer Corporation sold over $32 million worth of computer systems a day over the Internet. The consumer goes through an online configurator at www.dell.com to order a custom computer for home delivery. Many of the aforementioned products can be delivered right to the consumer's front door.

There are now many online shopping services for groceries and restaurant cuisine as well. Customers can use online grocery shopping services to create grocery lists and have a personal shopper pick out specific products (check out Peapod.com), redeem in-store coupons, and deliver the groceries right to the customer's residence. Many restaurants have had takeout and/or delivery with the phone; these same services are expanding to the Internet, too.

Gas stations and banks have evolved also. I can remember when I was a child that it was still routine to go to a full-service gas station and have an attendant pump gas, check oil and other fluid levels, tire pressure, etc. You never got out of the car. Today full-service stations are rare with the exception of states that require attendants to pump the gas. The norm at most gas stations is to have a large bank of self-service pumps that also have the option for self-payment at the pump. This fits in nicely with people's need to have more control of their time. As a customer, it is actually very empowering. I pull up to an available pump, pump the gas, and pay at the pump with a credit or debit card. I've shaved several minutes off a typical full-service fill-up. Gas stations can save labor costs as well by having one or two people run a large station. The Wayne Division of Dresser Equipment Group (see www.wayne.com) is helping to streamline this process even more. The Wayne Division created a system called Wayne TRAC (Transponder Activation System) that uses either car-mounted transponders or key chain transponders to validate a user's credit card information. If I have one of these transponders in my car and pull up to a gas station equipped with the TRAC system, my credit card approval process is already complete when I get out of the car. I just start pumping the gas… and leave.

Let's look at banks. Banks used to be high-touch low-convenience operations. Do you need to deposit a check? Go see the teller. Do you need to get a loan? Go see a loan administrator/officer. Do you need to get something notarized? Go see the office manager in the bank. Do you need to do any of these things before 9:00 a.m.? Well, you know the story… you're out of luck. However, the banking industry realized that they could provide nearly continuous support for most of the routine tasks of banking such as deposits, withdrawals, transfers, account balance information, and even stamp sales (in some locations) with ATMs. The kicker was there wouldn't be any additional labor required (many ATM operations are outsourced) and the customer gets a tremendous amount of control of his or her banking needs. Plus ATMs have enabled banks to expand their operations into new convenient locations such as markets, malls, movie theaters, and airports. The latest spin in the banking world is Internet banking. If you have an Internet account and the necessary software application (Quicken, Microsoft Money, or proprietary bank software) you can pay bills electronically, transfer money between accounts, check account balances, and a host of other activities. All of these activities increase the amount of self-service available to the end user.

I could continue to share many examples of on-demand products and services that are permeating our society. Many factors are fueling this need for instantaneous service and support. Technology is ever changing and providing opportunities for many improvements in cycle-time, efficiencies, and the capabilities of the tools, systems, hardware, and software we use. Work is more demanding now than it has ever been. Each person has more work to accomplish with less resources as companies re-engineer, downsize, rightsize, and so forth. People want to spend less time doing those things that are seen as menial. This is one of the reasons the services industry is expected to be one of the highest growth industries in the coming decade. Time is going to be a precious commodity in the coming millennium and the more people can do things they want, when they want, the more empowered they will feel. As James Gleick said in *Faster*, "Sociologists in several countries have found that increasing wealth and increasing education bring a sense of tension about time. We believe that we possess too little of it: that is a myth we live by now. What is true is that we are awash in things, in information, in news, in the rubble and shiny new toys of our complex civilization, and — strange, perhaps — stuff means speed. The wave patterns of all these facts and choices flow and crash about us at a heightened frequency. We live in the buzz" (Gleick, p. 10).

So, how does this relate to learning? What does it all mean? Learners will start to gravitate towards those solutions in which they are in control. It is going to get harder and harder for us to tell learners that they have to go to classroom 215 on the main campus between 9:00 a.m. until 10:00 a.m. Mondays, Wednesdays, and Fridays to learn about physical science. Less and less people are going to want to tune into the local public television station on Monday evenings at 6:00 p.m. to learn about American History or Finance for Non-Financial Managers.

Business leaders in corporations are pushing back more and more on pulling valuable sales representatives, technical support personnel, and managers away from the workplace to attend training in classrooms because of the opportunity costs associated with these people being away from their primary work tasks. This doesn't even begin to touch the capital and operating expenses associated with designing, developing, delivering, and evaluating traditional training in a brick and mortar classroom. To be viewed as business partners, learning practitioners must fundamentally change the way they think about learning. Employees are going to be drawn towards learning solutions that are at the desktop, on the shop floor, and where the work is. If possible it should be portable, reusable, accessible, and may often be disposable. It should be offered up in the smallest chunks possible. We must go from being best in class to best *out* of class.

The primary goals of this book are to increase the awareness of the coming autonomous learning movement and to provide examples of successful autonomous learning in action. As you read this book, compare examples of self-directed learning to traditional training you may currently be providing. One other area this book will provide insight to is the growing number of corporations that are providing customer training. This new group of learners that businesses will now have to educate will also demand the same ease of access and usability for *learning* they will have while using products and services. Mentally break down the highly structured learning event into the smallest learning bytes possible. Now offer them in a variety of media and in a variety of methods in a continuous learning *process*. You're well on your way to enabling enlightenment in the coming millennium.

Learning Byte   *Watch children in a pre-school or kindergarten at play if you want to see some examples of on-demand learning. Watch how each object or toy is picked up, tasted, pulled, tugged, licked, twisted, thrown, sat on, etc., until its secrets are uncovered.*

Some Highlights in Learning History

In order to discover where we are headed, it is often very valuable to take a retrospective look at where we have been. Practices that may have been necessary and/or valuable in previous centuries probably don't fit as well in today's on-demand culture. However, there is another reason to review an abridged history of some of the high points of education. Some people are going to need a bridge to get them over the troubling waters of on-demand learning. There is a large part of the population who will have a difficult time not being explicitly directed in their learning. So, we help these folks by providing some remnants of traditional classroom or other form of directed learning. For example, if we are going to have participants use a web-based training tool to learn about sales, then we might have them log into the system at a regularly scheduled time to interact with other participants or the instructor. This provides the *comfort* and *nudging* that some people need to get engaged with self-study. The technological advances we've had in the last ten to twenty years negate the need for some of the event-centric learning that is still the dominant learning paradigm in many cultures. This chapter provides a synopsis of key players and educational philosophies that we've used since the philosophical explosion created by the Greeks as early as the fifth century BC.

The Greeks Begin to Philosophize

The Greeks pushed the envelope on human thought and learning as early as 2,500 years ago. The Greeks were the first society to believe in and support a growing confidence in rational conscious enquiry. "If civilization is advance towards the control of mentality and environment by reason, then the Greeks did more for it than any of their other predecessors. They invented the philosophical question as part and parcel of one of the greatest intuitions of all time, that a coherent and logical explanation of things could be found, that the world did not ultimately rest upon the meaningless and arbitrary fiat of gods or demons" (Roberts, p. 192). This may seem insignificant in today's society, however, this was a quantum leap in rational thought that helped forge a way of learning.

Plato and the Academy

Plato, an aristocratic Athenian who published the first textbook on philosophy, called *The Republic*, created a place for learning outside the walls of Athens around 387 BC called the *Academy*. The Academy, probably the first university, was in the midst of an olive grove, a park, and a statue of the Greek hero Academus. Plato met with scholars from Greece and discussed mathematics, philosophy, natural science, and preparation for statesmanship. The Academy existed until approximately 529 AD when Justinian closed it and other pagan schools of the time. It was one of the early examples of people coming together in a central physical location to learn. People met with Plato (and the subsequent leaders of the Academy) at appointed times to learn. So the paradigm of classroom- and instructor-centric learning has been with us for nearly 2,400 years. This is one of the challenges associated with creating on-demand learning opportunities — our history.

Aristotle Creates the Lyceum

Plato's most famous student, Aristotle, was a great classifier and collector of data, especially in the area of biology. Aristotle used inductive arguments to prove points. His writings formed the framework for many future studies in areas such as physics, biology, and psychology. He was also the creator of deductive logic. Aristotle created the *Lyceum*, which was another advanced school of philosophy. Aristotle's students and followers were called *Peripatetics*. The name may be derived from Aristotle's custom of walking about (*peripatein*) while lecturing, or from the *peripatos* ("covered walk") of the Lyceum, the parklike area outside Athens where he lectured. People were beginning to take more control of their environments and using them to solve problems and unravel some of the mysteries of the universe.

Gutenburg Creates the Printing Press

One of the most important societal events to occur in our history was the development of the movable type printing press. Johannes Gutenberg (1394? – 1468) was a goldsmith who developed the printing press in the 1430s. He helped disperse the written word to many people. There are still copies of Gutenburg's Bibles in existence today. Gutenberg perfected his movable type and press systems to create books, pamphlets, and propaganda which catalyzed the development and spread of new ideas in the world.

John Amos Comenius Uses Pictures to Facilitate Learning

Comenius was a Czech educational reformer and religious leader who lived 1592–1670. He was educated at the University of Heidelberg. He was a teacher and rector in the Moravian towns of Prerov and Fulnek until the start of the Thirty Years' War, when the army of the Holy Roman Empire drove the Moravians into exile.[1] Comenius' major claim to fame was the use of pictures in his books to facilitate learning. His book, *Visible World in Pictures* (1658), a book to learn Latin, is believed to be the first illustrated textbook for children.

This was no small feat. Most textbooks used today continue in the example established by Comenius. Look at a child's textbook to see how prolific and colorful the illustration and photographs are inside the covers. Visual imagery streamlines the learning process and makes even potentially difficult theories and concepts easy to understand. Furthermore, visual imagery is not language dependent.

For example, I was asked back in college to write a paper on economics, and I was absolutely dreading it. So, I went to the library and started pulling out different books on economics and found a book on Japanese economics (*Japan, Inc.: An Introduction to Japanese Economics*) that was in fact a comic book (or *Manga*). I didn't realize it, but about one third of the publishing industry in Japan is done in comic books. They are used for entertainment, for education, for politics, for information, and for a variety of other reasons. People eight to eighty read them. Anyway, I was

---

[1] "Comenius, John Amos," *Microsoft® Encarta® 98 Encyclopedia.* ©1993-1997 Microsoft Corporation.

able to write my paper on Japanese economics using this book as the reference. Then, I got the idea to build a comic book for training where we worked. It took several months to complete, but it was a project I was passionate about. Primary research we conducted showed that it was very effective for retention of learning and also much more likely to be re-read. Friends of mine sent me Japanese textbooks (with no English translations) that I could start to decipher, just by seeing the pictures. So, it is easy to see that the combination of text and words that John Amos Comenius initiated in 1658 has had a powerful and lasting affect on us as learners even today.

John Dewey

John Dewey was a professional educator who lived between 1859 and 1952. His breakthrough principle in learning theory was that children learn best when their lessons are related to the real world. He disagreed with the prevalent practice of the day, which was to use rote learning and abstract theorizing. He wanted children to learn to think critically using analysis and logic. He didn't see the value in learning ideas and information out of their social context. One ironic point about Mr. Dewey

© 1999 King Features Syndicate; Reprinted with special permission of King Features Syndicate.

was that he was less than riveting in the classroom. As a person who touted creating interest in the classroom, he had trouble doing it.

How do the tenets of John Dewey relate to on-demand learning? First of all, when we are learning on-demand, as we need to, when we want to, then we don't want or need to learn unrelated information and knowledge not contextually related to the job at hand. If I need to know how to drive a car, I can learn this skill without knowledge of how the car was built, internal combustion theory, or even automobile repair. Additionally, I think that more and more secondary schools and colleges are going to migrate to offering increasing levels of skill-based training. Corporations spend billions of dollars a year assimilating newly hired people in skills that secondary schools and colleges have either diluted with theory or bypassed completely. Eventually, corporations will help force change in collegiate curricula, or alternative solutions will be born to meet the needs of business.

Behaviorism

B. F. Skinner (1904 – 1990) was the founder of the theory of behaviorism. Behaviorism's primary tenet is that humans react primarily to environmental stimuli and not to ideas or their subconscious desires. Thus people (and other animals) can be taught things with positive reinforcement. Skinner invented a series of devices to facilitate his studies of behavior and his theories were heavily followed in the 1950s and 1960s. Behaviorism carried over into learning as well.

Summary

I've reviewed a series of events in learning history that relate to the way people have learned through the ages. There are elements of many of these activities that are still valuable today. We can use aspects of key teachings and methods and pull the best of these together into a more powerful homogeneous mixture. It is also crucial to remember that people have endured nearly continuous classroom or group-centric learning for ages. Knowing this will help you understand why people may push back so hard when you want to migrate to a more self-directed, learner-centric continuous learning model. Stand your ground … push back appropriately, and offer as many alternatives as feasible, and soon you will have people demanding to get out of the classroom.

The On-Demand Learner

To facilitate behavioral changes in employees, customers, and other people who need to do things differently, it's helpful to review the makeup of the average adult learner. What makes the adult learner tick? What competencies are evident in the on-demand learner? What societal and technological changes are going to affect the way the on-demand learner gathers, analyzes, and synthesizes the information he or she receives? This chapter provides a profile of the on-demand learner and a checklist for action for purveyors of learning. It identifies strategies to maximize the effectiveness of on-demand learning solutions and provides ways to match learners with solutions that will work today and tomorrow.

Time is a valuable commodity. There never seems to be enough time, even though time as we perceive it stays constant. There are twenty-four hours in a day (give or take very slight variations from year to year), just as there have been for thousands of years. The reason so many people feel that they "don't have enough time" during the day to get things accomplished is because everyone is trying to do so much more in the day. People are so much more connected with cell phones, pagers, the Internet, and so forth, that it affects the perception of time. People can be reached anywhere, any time, which erodes the boundaries of work, home, and leisure activities. Also, there are many distractions that are available around the clock. People can watch dozens of cable or satellite channels on their televisions continuously through the day and night. The Internet is alive and well in an electronic buzz... non-stop. Many employees are responsible for more at the work site as their jobs are expanded (the actual organizational developmental definition of this phenomena is called *horizontal loading*). Familial and social responsibilities are extremely demanding as well. There are soccer practices, school meetings, grocery shopping, karate classes, choir practices, and hundreds of other responsibilities to help pull many people in divergent directions and add stress. So, we really don't have less time in the day, but we are all trying to pack so much more into it. It's like trying to shove 70 pounds of oranges into a sack designed to hold 40 pounds. The bag may hold all of the oranges, but it may be weakened, or stretch, or break. All of the aforementioned issues support the notion of on-demand learning. Since time is so valuable, it follows that people will want to use their time as wisely as possible. The end user of the learning would much rather be able to get the learning when he or she needs it and in manageable sessions that don't monopolize his or her time.

Adult Learning Principles

Adults have some special qualities that can and should be leveraged when we talk about creating on-demand learning opportunities.

Adults Are Self-Directed

Adult learners are self-directed. Contrast this with children, who generally have to be told what and why they need to learn things. Adults can take charge of their learning and use strategies and methods best suited to their own situation. Furthermore, large parts of the adult workforce are knowledge workers, and knowledge workers already configure their day-to-day work. This adult learning principle ties itself nicely to the notion of on-demand learning. Adults self-direct their learning and will go get the learning they need. If we provide on-demand or just-in-time learning interventions, the self-directed aspect of adult learners parallels nicely with how adults naturally learn.

Adults Have Rich Experience Bases

Experience plays a key role in the adult learner when contrasted with the way children learn. Schoolage children do not have the large experience base that most adults have. Children are building their experience banks in these formative years. So, when teaching children, it can be difficult to try to relay similar activities (or experiences) to provide a learning bridge. For example, if we are going to teach a group of adults how to drive a tractor, we could relate the experience of driving a car to provide some similar examples to help streamline the learning process. If we said to a group of third graders, "Starting a tractor is like starting a car, you put the key in the ignition, and then turn it," the reference point makes no sense. Most third-grade children have not started cars. The way the role of experience relates to on-demand learning solutions is that creators of on-demand learning solutions should take advantage of the experiences adults have when designing solutions. Using analogies and/or thematic approaches in learning solutions that tie to experiences that most adults have will streamline the learning process even more.

Adults Have Different Kinds of Experiences

As people grow older, the experience base they have gets more diverse. There is a tremendous amount of variability in their experience bases. Children conversely have similar kinds of experience and relate to similar situations relative to the limited number of experiences they have had. This is something to consider when implementing on-demand learning solutions. Analyze your target audience well when you get ready to design your solution so that you can take advantage of the variability in the end users' experiences. Provide a variety of ways to access the solution: provide scenarios that vary in depth and breadth. Allow people to go as shallow or deep into a learning solution as possible and provide a variety of ways for people to navigate when using a tool.

Adults Need to Be Motivated

There is a common acronym in the training and learning arena that every training designer, developer, and deliverer has seen. It's WIIFM (aka WIFM), or What's In It For Me? As an adult, I've already got plenty of distractions, demands, and responsibilities on my hands. I am not going to stand for "extra" or "fluff" training that will not provide a tangible benefit to my family or myself. If I'm an accountant and I need to get forty hours of continuous learning units per year to maintain my certification, I have a very strong motivation to get the learning. Children, on the other hand, will learn just about anything, whether or not it is related to specific activities that they have to do. Think about all of the things that we "learned" over the years as schoolchildren that are no more than trivia (and worse, since we can't remember most of what we "learned" anyway). Roger Schank stated it well: "The gap between what I learned about learning and how and what children are taught in school was enormous. As I watched my children go through school, I was amazed at the way in which the schools taught them. They were just as bored as I was, but now I could analyze the problem. They were being called upon to memorize many useless facts under stressful conditions, information they promptly forgot the following year when they had to memorize a new set of useless learning. They were being told what to learn independent of their desire to know it" (Schank, p. xi). How does motivation play into the design and development of on-demand learning solutions? First and foremost is the requirement that the learning solution will at least facilitate development of motivation to use and learn the knowledge needed. Always try to provide blatant WIIFMs in the on-demand learning solution to catalyze the desire to learn and to get the necessary mindshare of the target audience to ensure that the solution is used.

Adults Need a Social Context for Their Learning

Besides having a need for motivation in their learning, adults need to have a social context for what is learned. "Context analysis is concerned with the influences on the setting in which the learning occurs as well as where learners are likely to apply what they learn" (Galbraith, p. 10). Galbraith goes on to say, "Adults have perceptions of standards, expectations, and opportunities that are directly related to their purpose for learning. Understanding these perceptions allows the learner and you to contribute to the decisions on 'using learning activities to strengthen problem solving, specifying mastery levels, and helping learners use educational strategies that enable them to use or deflect influences that encourage or discourage them to learn and apply.'" When you recognize the various contextual influences an organization has, you can plan and implement learning solutions that will lead to more meaningful learning experiences for the learner.

On-Demand Learners Are Flexible And Open to Using New Learning Practices

On-demand learners realize the value and power of having control of their learning including how it is done, when it is scheduled, and getting access to it. Many of these people are juggling complex work and home lives and are thankful for opportunities to allocate learning in the time and place most appropriate for them. They are hungry to get the knowledge and skills necessary and don't cringe at the thought of using a variety of modalities to learn. One really great example of this is the advent of nontraditional for-profit universities that are cropping up. Examples of these include the University of Phoenix (owned by the Apollo Group Inc.), DeVry Inc., ITT Educational Services Inc., Caliber Learning Network, Jones International University, and more than 1,600 corporate universities across the United States.

Let's take a closer look at one of the more widely known nontraditional universities: the University of Phoenix. The University of Phoenix was founded in 1976 with eight students. Today nearly 62,000 adults are enrolled, which makes the University of Phoenix the largest private university in the United States. Students are allowed to concentrate on one class at a time, if they like, and learn from their homes. The classes are sequenced so they can more readily meet the needs of the degree the students are seeking. Classes are repeated often, so participants can temporarily refrain from attending classes as work and other issues arise. Contrast this with many traditional universities that may schedule certain necessary classes every third or fourth semester. This means if you miss a class needed for your degree program, you might have to wait more than a year to take it, to potentially complete the degree. The draw for many University of Phoenix students is flexible, convenient, efficient customer service that meets their needs.

Knowledge Worker versus Blue-collar Worker (Prefigured vs. Configured Work)

The workforce is transitioning and will continue to transition into the next millennium. Hundreds of years ago, most people worked using their hands to till the soil, or complete craftwork, or work in mines, and many other types of manual labor. The Industrial Revolution catalyzed the industrial plant worker and the theories and practices around scientific management (á la Frederick Taylor, who used scientific management practices to wring out every possible efficiency in factory work processes). These blue-collar workers or laborers, generally, had their work prefigured for them. That is, the steps, tools, systems, and work relationships were already created. The workers did not have to think about how to complete their tasks. Step 1 is *always...Place the widget into the gizmo*. Step two is *always…Polish the doodad*, and so forth. The work is already figured out, or prefigured.

Move the clock forward to the new millennium. Most people in the workforce are knowledge workers and have to configure their work. Think about your job. If you are a white-collar worker, you are probably doing lots of *project* work. Project work can be completed by several groups of professionals in a variety of ways, but can still end up with the desired outcome. Your boss or team leader probably doesn't say, "Mark, I want you to win the Stratos account by calling the marketing department, flying to Denver, creating a proposal, providing status reports, creating a solid team.…" Mark is probably told, "You need to win the Stratos account by the end of the next fiscal quarter." The implications here are powerful.

People in prefigured work are more used to having prescriptive training guidance. They are used to being told exactly what to learn, how to learn it, when to learn it, where to learn it, and so forth. They may have a hard time when they are asked to undertake more self-directed learning. This doesn't mean that they can't be coached to do this, it just means that the pre-existing propensity to learn is probably going to be instructor-centered instead of learner-centered.

Contrast this to configured workers who have to *configure* or create their work on a daily basis. Certainly, some things are routine and occur with limited regularity, but the nature of project work generally entails different stakeholders, teams, business problems, timelines, etc. The configured worker will not have many projects that are repeatable because of the nature of project work. In this sense, the configured worker (aka the knowledge worker) should be more open to learning with a variety of methods, including self-directed ways, to get the necessary upleveling in skills required.

In my own job, this has been absolutely true. I've worked on more than fifty projects in the last three or four years and can honestly say that no two have been alike. There's always some process change, or organizational change, or change in the original solution request to help make it interesting. Also true is the fact that I like being able to take charge of my learning. I've never liked having to wait to get registered, and waiting for the class time to happen, and having to wait for other people to go get things that I could have learned on my own with the right set of tools and feedback in place.

Multitasking and Multilearning

Bill Gates said, "Business is going to change more in the next ten years than it has in the last fifty" (Gates, p. xiii). This means that the rate of change in the business arena is going to increase much more than it has in the past half-century. New products are rolling out faster, business relationships and agreements are made (and broken) quicker, and working folks can't just keep up with their jobs, because their entire business world is evolving, too. At a higher level, mergers, leveraged buyouts, and initial public offerings blanket the business landscape and increase the complexity of businesses and those who work in them. The term *multitasking* is generally used to describe computer operations. In the coming millennium, the sheer rate of business change will cause most *people* to become multitaskers. Downsizing, reengineering, job sharing, and horizontal loading will heighten the multitasking effect, too. Those folks who cannot multitask will find it more difficult to succeed in the future.

One of my favorite nonwork examples of this is the way television shows and networks have changed the face of what is displayed on the television screen. It used to be that we rarely saw titles or text on the television screen, with the exception of the opening and closing credits. Newscasters would have their names shown below them in a small font for a brief moment in time. Network icons and logos were used in separate advertising. (Remember how the major non-cable networks used to actually have ads.) Contrast this with today's television environments. Pick up your remote and tune into CNBC™ around lunchtime. The viewing area is dissected by text, scrolling figures in a variety of colors, charts, graphics, and don't forget the omnipresent translucent network icon. Somewhere in one of the corners of the screen you will see an analyst talking. The same is true of QVC and many other stations as well. There is a veritable information overload on the television twenty-four hours a day. Fifteen years ago, people would have screamed about a visual assault like this. Now with the advent of the Internet, web browsers, MTV, Windows™ software, video games, and the pace of information transfer, we can handle very busy television screens.

The implications for the on-demand learner and for the creator of on-demand learning opportunities are powerful. People are going to be pulled and stretched and challenged at work and home in a variety of ways. So, we who create these learning catalysts must facilitate multilearning. Multilearning is learning a multitude of knowledge and skills simultaneously. If you think about it, that's how most of us learn the things we need to know in order to do our jobs. Every day we are learning bits and pieces of what makes up the holistic puzzle of job knowledge. Picture a sales representative. Wherever she works, she has to learn the products and/or services she is selling. She must learn about her company. She must learn who to include in her network so that she can get things done. Then there are company initiatives, new products, ethics training, and compliance training, ad infinitum. It's inconceivable to think that she'll learn all of these things at scheduled times in a classroom. So, create multilearning opportunities. Create these opportunities so they can be used at just the right time and they will be used.

Competencies of the On-Demand Learner

"Competencies are underlying characteristics of people and indicate ways of behaving or thinking, generalizing across situations, and enduring for a reasonably long period of time" (Spencer, p. 9). In order for an individual to perform jobs at an appropriate level, he or she must possess the requisite competencies for the position. If a position called "On-Demand Learner" existed, it would include the following competencies:

Results Oriented

On-demand learners are driven by a need for results. They want to improve themselves and make their lives more successful and enjoyable. An obvious way for a person to achieve personal results is to engage in self-directed learning activities.

Takes Initiative

On-demand learners exhibit a disposition toward action. They are proactive and don't mind doing more than the minimum activity required to reach a goal. This meshes perfectly with the typical self-directed learning opportunities that people use to better themselves.

Information Seeking

Another common competency for on-demand learners is information seeking. On-demand learners are information hounds ... or maybe packrats is a better word. They gather all the information they can, scan it, filter it, and use it when they can. Sometimes this happens immediately. If not, the on-demand learner has information retrieval systems built in to use the information when needed.

I find this competency very strongly in myself. I am always reading something, or surfing the web, or talking to people, asking questions, probing, and looking for ways that information can be reassembled in ways that haven't been conceived previously. It's interesting and valuable to see how apparently nonrelated concepts or relationships often can be melded together in a new more powerful relationship. This is a valuable skill because it helps spawn innovation and directly supports the notion of on-demand learning.

Demonstrates Self-Efficacy

Having the confidence in one's abilities to do something is very important. That's what self-efficacy is all about. If a person doesn't fundamentally believe that he or she can do something by him- or herself, then it will be difficult for the person to complete the desired task. For instance, if I want to learn how to play tennis, but I am unconfident about my ability to learn it, I will have problems playing tennis. Think about it. If I really believe I am a terrible player, I will be less likely to practice and I will be very unlikely to play anyone better than me. It is important to play people better in order to make mistakes and *to learn*. So, an on-demand learner is confident in his or her abilities to learn in a self-directed or non-traditional method.

Self-efficacy is a powerful competency to possess and probably one of the most difficult to develop when it comes to people's perceived ability to learn by themselves. Learners have been brainwashed so long that many of them don't feel like they can learn unaided. Those who know they can make better on-demand learners.

Demonstrates Flexibility

On-demand learners should be flexible. True on-demand learning is going to occur in many ways and in fact some of the learning will be unintentional. The flexible person realizes this and is ready to capture knowledge in a variety of ways.

Learns on the Fly

This competency almost goes without saying. On-demand learning is all about learning things on the fly, just in time, just when it is needed. People with this competency can extract learning bytes and use them as they need to. These folks don't need to go to a five-day class to get crucial information and/or skills to do their jobs more efficiently. They can learn on the fly and still continue to complete their required job tasks.

Goal Driven

People who can readily learn on-demand generally are able to establish clear short- and long-term goals. They formulate the goals, identify enabling activities to reach them, and will do whatever it takes to reach their desired states. Few things will deter these people when they are on a quest for the next accomplishment. This competency parallels the philosophy of on-demand learning, since autonomous learners can get the skills and knowledge they need when they need to in support of a goal.

Consider this scenario. You work for a start-up company that manufactures gizmos. You've been given an opportunity to fly to several Latin American companies in six weeks to make a presentation on the latest gizmo your company has developed. Marketing analysis has shown that the product will sell well in several of these countries. There's only one problem, you don't speak Spanish and the CEO wants you to make the presentation because of your technical and sales expertise. The deal could be a multimillion dollar windfall for the company (and a hefty commission for you) if you can make the right pitch. You call the local junior college in a panic to see what kind of Spanish classes you can get. Oops! The next session starts in two months. That's too late. There is one professional school for foreign language in your town. The class here starts in three weeks. Again, you start to panic... and then you remember the Internet. You go to some online bookstores and order some computer-based training (CBT) on Spanish. You also find a couple of pocket guides you can take with you and use as a reference. Finally, you find a small firm on the Internet that will translate your English slides into Spanish for a reasonable fee. Six weeks later you make your first presentation in Spanish and win the contract.

The focus on this short-term goal enabled the gizmo representative to seek out alternative learning methods to enable him to make the sale. Without the goal, there would have been no need to learn enough Spanish to make the presentation and subsequent sale, and thus there would have been no learning of a new and valuable skill.

Career Oriented

The on-demand learner has a strong focus on his or her career. Because most of our jobs change on a very regular basis, it is important that we can gain new skills, understand new relationships, and learn continuously. Those folks who are happy to languish in their current roles are less accepting of on-demand learning. If a person is not going to take initiative to set and strive to complete goals, it is difficult to believe that he or she is going to focus activity on self-directed learning activities necessary to advance his or her career.

Competency Map

So the competency map for the on-demand learner includes:

- Results Oriented
- Takes Initiative
- Information Seeking
- Demonstrates Self-Efficacy
- Demonstrates Flexibility
- Learns on the Fly
- Goal Driven
- Career Oriented

Summary

In this chapter you've read about the on-demand learner and how he or she learns. There was a brief review of some adult learning principles and how they should be considered when facilitating on-demand learning. The ability of on-demand learners to be flexible and to use alternative learning methods was discussed. Finally, the competency map for the on-demand learner was laid out.

In the next chapter, you will learn some tips and techniques to enable on-demand learning.

> **Learning Byte** *Tax time is a national period of on-demand learning (and mourning, I guess). The federal government and the Internal Revenue Service (IRS) change the rules every year, so we all get to "figure out" what we owe anew each year.*

How to Enable On-Demand Learning

So far I've discussed the on-demand society, I've reviewed a micro history of learning, and I've talked about competencies of the on-demand learner. In this section I am going to share ways that you can enable on-demand learning. Here I discuss philosophical and design issues associated with providing just-in-time solutions to your employees or to your customer base. As I've mentioned several times before (and will probably mention again), learners will begin to demand this type of learning from their schools, universities, government organizations, and corporations. The following are some of the things you should consider when you provide on-demand learning opportunities for the clients you serve.

Shatter Some Paradigms

One critical thing you will have to remember is that there are several learning paradigms (or myths) that you will clash with when you try to implement on-demand learning. The first one is that classrooms and instructors are still the optimal way for everybody to learn, and the second is that most students cannot handle self-study or self-directed learning and cannot get just the information they need (instead of the entire forty-hour course).

"Put me in a classroom with an instructor, I learn better that way."

As I shared with you in the chapter on learning history, students have been coming together in central physical locations at appointed times for nearly 2,400 years. Most schools, universities, and corporations have been using that model so long that many students get very uneasy when they are asked to learn in other ways. I've heard people say,

"I can't learn unless I'm in a classroom with an instructor." I don't believe this for one second. People cook gourmet meals, sail boats, repair complex car engines, coach soccer teams, and thousands of other tasks unaided by instructors. When's the last time you actually registered and paid for a class on completing a tax return? Tax returns can be pretty daunting and the penalties for not completing a return correctly can be costly. However, since this is an off-the-job task, the individual feels less threatened by reading and studying the tax forms and maybe calling a person for help on some important questions.

Somehow though, when people cross the threshold of the workspace in the morning, or swing, or midnight shift, it as if a big neon sign gets erected that says, "No Learning Alone Allowed Here!" A huge component of enabling on-demand learning is helping to educate people about self-efficacy and letting them know that they can in fact learn on their own... on the job, too.

One notion that you may have to consider when migrating to an on-demand learning environment is that people may actually have to learn how to learn again. Communication, education, and reaffirmation may be necessary to facilitate the movement towards on-demand learning. Coach and mentor people so they can have successful experiences in self-learning when they get started. This will increase the students' confidence for future learning opportunities. When I am considering using a new consultant to assist our team, I find a small project that I can use as a performance assessment. If the consultant handles the initial assignment well, he or she gets more complex (and larger dollar) projects. This allows for my assessment and a chance for the consultant to gain confidence and learn how things work inside our organization. Similarly, if students are just starting to learn using self-directed methodologies, every success will make the next learning experience easier and every success will expand the student's confidence level.

"Students won't take time to learn on their own and we've got to inundate them with theory."

I truly believe that people are much smarter than we think they are. John Coné, the Vice President of Dell Learning, explains it (as he often does) with a funny story.

At some point or another a manager is going to need to know how to complete a performance appraisal for his or her staff. So what happens? Instead of giving the new manager the job-aid on completing the performance appraisal, we send the manager to three days of performance management training. The new manager gets inundated with the theory behind performance management. The manager is shown various models with lots of arrows and boxes that hopefully are in a closed loop. Somewhere on the third day of the training, the manager finally gets a one-hour session (and gets to use the tool or performance support system) on how to complete the appraisal. Trainers and managers are too afraid to give the manager just what he or she needs to know. They seem to fear that to do so without hours or days of context and caveats represents great danger. Managers show the same fear in allowing people to learn just what they need to know that they would if they were told to *give chainsaws to children*.

Changing habits of people who have been socialized to learn only when directed by instructors can be challenging, but it is not impossible. I've found that if you can provide people *hybrid* learning opportunities, participants can often make the adjustment. What is a hybrid learning opportunity? It is when a tool, an electronic performance support system (EPSS), technology-enabled learning system, or any other kind of self-directed learning tool, is used in a classroom or lab setting. In this way, people get the sense they are still in a classroom, but they can use the tool and get help as needed. When they are back on the job, they will be better able to use the tool. As people get used to the non-classroom aspects of learning, training departments can start to wean learners from the classroom. This is called *fading*. Eventually, you will be able to release on-demand learning strategies as soon as they are developed. In fact, people will start to demand these new interventions as they see how empowered they become using them.

Make It Easier to Use and It Will Get Used

Many times it is said that people are resistant to change. This is somewhat, but not completely, true. People are very resistant to change that makes things harder. Often changes that are implemented actually are much more difficult to use or master than the previous tool or solution that was in place. Charles Handy, social philosopher and author, says that people can handle incremental change, i.e., change that occurs over a long period of time. He says that you can put a frog in water and slowly turn the heat up and it will boil to death (incremental change). If you put a similar frog into boiling water at the start, it would leap out immediately. This is an example of acute change. So, when we provide on-demand learning solutions for our clients, the intervention should ideally provide incremental versus acute change. It should be seamless for the user and should be as easy if not easier to use than the current offering(s). For example, if you currently have to go to a four-hour classroom compliance briefing, a 45-minute self-paced web tutorial for the same information would be something easier and less time consuming to accomplish. Therefore, it passes the easier-to-use test.

Make It Accessible

It may seem apparent, but whatever solutions are used, created, or offered, must be made accessible. You can have the slickest, most high-tech, gadget-laden learning solution that the planet has ever seen, but if your target audience hasn't seen it, hasn't heard of it, can't afford it, or can't get to it, it just doesn't matter. Your entire target audience for the solution must be able to get to it when they need to. That means they've got to know where it is, how to get to it, how to start it, and so forth.

This means that you have to do your needs assessments up front to determine what the lowest common denominator is in the group(s) you are trying to serve. If you are providing learning opportunities for a manufacturing organization that has very limited access to personal computers, it is probably wise to carefully consider any computer-based solutions you are contemplating. Are you considering sound in a web-based tool? Does the audience you're serving have sound cards and speakers in their systems? Will remote personnel be trying to log into an Intranet on a slow modem line? Are there security issues around information you want to put on an external server? Is the new web-based tool you've created easy to find or launch? Or do people have to spend ten minutes using a search engine to find it? There are many technical considerations in any solution that you build or buy.

There is one other issue associated with accessibility, and that is cost. I was asked one time by a client to create thirty-two hours of custom computer-based training (CBT) for an organization with twenty-six people in it. When I gave the manager a ballpark estimate for the finished CBT of $50,000 – $60,000 per hour for a total of $1.92 million, or roughly $71,000 per employee, she quickly realized that the amount grossly exceeded her entire annual training budget. We designed a less expensive but effective solution that was *accessible*. The bottom line is that if your bottom line is too high, it makes the learning solution inaccessible.

Build for the Lowest Common Denominator

Related to the accessibility of the learning are the design specifications that are used to build the learning solution. If none of the target audience for your solution has sound cards in their computers, it wouldn't be wise to design an on-demand learning solution that is dependent on sound through the computer. This may seem like a silly point, but learning organizations often do this. In elementary school, when the class is going to learn about recycling one gallon milk jugs by creating bird houses, scoops, and flower pots, the teacher sends a note home and asks students to bring a gallon milk container to school. This ensures that everyone starts on the same level. The curriculum is built around the lowest common denominator or, in this case, insurance that all students start with the same raw materials. It is very easy to get swept away by promises from zealous sales personnel about how various technology-enabled solutions will become the panacea of training and learning in your organization. However, if the intended audience doesn't have the minimum required technology, media, or tools, the solution will not be as effective as it could be. Now, does this mean that if there is no standardization of learning and/or computer systems in your organization that you can't implement a new learning methodology? No. It does mean that you will have to create alternatives that allow the lowest common denominator of technology to have access to the tool. In the case of a new system that requires sound, it could be as simple as providing a text-based summary of the same content. One could also deliver the sound through another medium such as a prerecorded cassette or CD that accompanies the solution.

Provide Feedback Junkies a Fix

Another way to help enable on-demand learning is to provide multiple opportunities for feedback to the learner. One of the key reasons that much on-demand or self-directed or technology-enabled instruction fails is because it lacks the rich feedback that the average classroom provides. Think about it. In a classroom, there is regular feedback from the instructor (if he or she is a decent facilitator). Participants provide feedback to questions you ask, comments you make, and questions the instructor has. There is sensory feedback in the classroom related to temperature, lighting, color, olfactory, and textural cues. Social feedback occurs continually during the classroom session as jokes are told, eye contact is made, body language is exchanged, love or hate for the instructor develops, and so forth. Engaging activities can be used such as games, role-plays, project work, small group discussion, and opportunities to practice blossoming skills. People eat this stuff up. It's nearly a continuous feedback stream during a good classroom session. Now compare that with some of the typical web-enabled or computer-based training that you've seen. It is often mindless clicking of a forward arrow to advance the next text-based slide with cookie-cutter clip art that doesn't relate to the text. So, to enable on-demand learning, especially when using technology, it is imperative that there are multiple opportunities for feedback built in to the solution. You must quench the need for feedback or your solution will not be used.

I think about web sites that I frequent. My favorite sites are those that allow me to input data and receive a product as a result of *my input*. For example, I need to get from my house in Pflugerville, Texas, to a car dealership in Abilene, Texas, but I don't know how to get there. Well, I can go to Mapblast.com and enter my address and the street address of the car dealership. One mouse click later I've got a map with door-to-door text directions to get there. I've acted on the web site and it's provided me a product. When I go to Amazon.com I get a welcome from the company with a list of recommended reading based on where I live and also based on previous purchases I've made. When I enter a book order, I get a book delivered to my door within a couple of days. These are great examples of sites that are interactive and provide feedback. If you don't input the right information, you will end up in the wrong place or get the wrong book sent to your house, or receive no book at all. Think about ways you can add this type of feedback to your on-demand learning solutions for all of the feedback junkies (including you) out there.

Allow Plenty of Practice Time — It's Like Riding a Unicycle

When you are designing on-demand learning opportunities, it is important that you allow people to practice using the knowledge they need or the skills that you want them to perform — often. One year for Christmas (I think it was 1973 when I was ten and in the fourth grade), my parents asked my brother and I what we wanted to get from Santa

Claus. My brother, Stephen, and I had learned to walk on stilts that my father had built for us and we were ready for our next skill-building challenge. We decided that we both wanted to get unicycles (we could already ride bicycles). On Christmas morning that year, we discovered that Santa had amazingly delivered the unicycles to our small house in Meridian, Mississippi <wink wink, nudge nudge>. Stephen and I were thrilled. We couldn't wait to ride them! Now, in case you're wondering, the unicycles came with no instructions or tips, and of course my parents didn't know how to ride them, so they couldn't tell us (i.e., lecture us) how to ride these one-wheeled contraptions. But we were determined to learn to ride these things. The unicycles came with two poles similar to what a downhill skier uses to help maintain balance. After nearly impaling ourselves with the poles, Stephen and I threw them to the side and just started using our arms to balance. We quickly learned through some nasty falls that it was best to learn this skill on the grass and not on the asphalt. We also quickly discovered that one of the hardest things to do on a unicycle is to get up on it. So we held on to a tree and got upright on the unicycles that way. After many attempts, falls, and bruises we found we could actually push off and go about four or five feet before we fell. Another round of practice told us the importance of four-way balance. On a unicycle you must be able to balance to your left and right (like on a bicycle) and also forward and backwards. One of the most important things we learned about unicycle riding, again through extensive practice, is that once you start, you cannot stop pedaling until you are ready to stop the unicycle. This is very different from a chain-driven bicycle that allows you to stop pedaling and coast. If you stop pedaling on a unicycle you stop, unless you rock back and forth on it. Stephen and I actually got good enough through the extensive practice that we could ride the unicycles as long as we wanted. We even played basketball on them, delivered newspapers, and other things. I still have a Schwinn unicycle to this day; it's in my attic. Every once in a while I pull it out and put air in the tire and show my son (and myself) that I can still ride it. The reason I can still ride it is because of the extensive practice that was needed to learn the skill the first time. In a similar vein, for your on-demand learning solutions to be as powerful as possible, you should build as much practice into the solution as possible. *Telling someone* how to do something is never as powerful as *letting him or her do it*. So build as many practice opportunities into on-demand learning activities as you can create.

Allow People to Fail in a Safe Environment

Roger Schank wrote an interesting book called *Virtual Learning* (1997). One of the major premises of this book is that true learning does not take place unless there are built-in opportunities for end-users of the learning solution to fail. Failure, of course, has negative connotations.

> The F word (failure) is anathema to both teachers and CEOs. We punish students with bad grades when they offer the wrong answers on tests. We punish employees with negative performance reviews when they make mistakes. The bigger the failure, the bigger the punishment: Flunking and termination await those who fail frequently. (Schank, p. 29)

The ironic thing about this is that allowing people to fail in a safe, nonthreatening environment is one of the most powerful learning enablers around.

> Consider what happens when learners' expectations are met. For instance, when they sit down to work at their desks they always manage to land in their chairs. Because their expectations are met, they don't have to think about or explain sitting down. But what would happen if one day they sat down and landed on the floor, missing the chair? They would have to think about and explain the failure. The outcome leads to two guiding principles of failure:
>
> - Real thinking never starts until the learner fails.
> - It is easy to recognize their expectation failures because people insist on explaining them.
>
> Thinking and explaining catalyze learning. (Schank, p. 31)

What are some ways that you can provide opportunities for people to fail in a nonthreatening environment? How are you using assessments in your training and learning programs?

Use Assessments to Direct Learning - Not to Punish

At every place I have worked in my career from the U.S. Navy to various private corporations, testing has been used. In the case of the Navy, there was extensive knowledge testing, performance-based testing, oral boards, and operational experience required (rightly so, since I was a nuclear power plant operator) to be an effective member of my crew. In some of the other places I've worked, in much less hazardous positions, I've had some difficult testing on areas such as ethics, company mission and vision statements, and other nonlife-threatening topical areas. There were many tests issued at some organizations I've worked that were unnecessary and really an exercise in short-term memory. I couldn't pass many of those knowledge tests now if I had to. When you use assessments, you must have a good reason to create and use them. The assessment items should be based on learning objectives that are tied to *necessary job performance.* And again, the results of the assessments should not be used in a punitive nature. That is, the results of a test should not be used as the basis of not hiring or firing someone, increasing someone's pay, or lowering a performance rating. The only exception to this rule is if a local, state, or federal requirement has deemed a certification necessary. Of course, if this is true then the tests will be checked for validity and reliability using statistical analyses and psychometric review.

Psychometricians are experts in test item construction and test validity and reliability who you can use to assist in this area if you don't have the expertise in-house. Colleges with education psychology departments are good sources for these people if you need testing services.

At Dell, we have come up with a strict policy on use of assessments. Assessments will primarily be used to direct learning. The learner can focus on those areas that he or she was weakest in to improve them. We also use them as a way to revise our curriculum, make program learning changes, and so forth. We never use them as a punitive tool. Since many on-demand learning solutions are self-directed and paced, assessments can provide valuable roadmaps for learning. Again, in on-demand learning solutions, the assessments should provide the navigation of the learning to occur, not to punish or ridicule.

Break Content Down to the Smallest Possible Chunk

A basic tenet about on-demand learning is to provide it in the smallest possible chunk. There are several reasons for this. When learning is broken down into its smallest division (sometimes referred to as a learning byte, object, chunk, etc.) it can quickly be transferred to the person who needs it. If it is a short passage of text or a definition of a word or a picture, this learning byte can quickly be passed to the learner. The object is small in size and can be easily distributed by a network to a learner's desktop. Also, when content is broken down into the smallest possible chunks, it is easier to create an á la carte lesson or module. The designer can pull a series of learning objects together to create a custom learning module.

Get Learners What They Need as Quickly as Possible

I've mentioned many times the need for on-demand learning. On-demand learning implies access to the necessary learning tools now, not tomorrow, sometime next week, or next month — but right now. Think about times that you've been connected with the friendly VRU, or Voice Response Unit, on the telephone. You call your bank to find the answer to a simple question. How much money was direct deposited in my account today? The communication goes something like this:

> Hello and welcome to the Anyplace Bank's interactive voice system. You can get current account information by responding to a series of simple questions.... Listen closely, our menu has recently changed. If you want this message in Spanish, select 2 now. ...If you want information on your savings account, push 1 now. Checking account, push 2. Loan information 3... ad infinitum. (This is where the customer starts getting irritated.) Now to get information about a recent check that has cleared, press 1. To get information about your balance, press 2. To get information on your four most recent deposits, push 3. Blah Blah Blah....." My heart rate is increasing now, I am pacing the floor in circles like a caged animal. Finally, after entering account numbers, passwords, and secret handshakes, I get the information I wanted about five minutes ago.

Like the example above, it is easy to frustrate and confuse the very people we are trying to help by taking people indirectly to the information or skills they crave. Get the learning solutions to the people in as few steps as possible. It will streamline the learning process as well as minimize frustration levels.

Summary

To summarize some of the main points about enabling on-demand learning, remember:

- Shatter some paradigms
- Get out of the classroom
- Allow the student to take charge of his or her own learning
- Make it easier to use and it will get used
- Make it accessible
- Build for the lowest common denominator
- Provide feedback junkies a fix

- Allow plenty of practice time – it's like riding a unicycle
- Allow people to fail in a safe environment
- Use assessments to direct learning – not to punish
- Break content down to the smallest possible chunk
- Get learners what they need as quickly as possible.

If you can implement some of these tenets, you will see growth in learner satisfaction, since the learner will now be in command.

In the next chapter, I discuss some of the technological considerations for on-demand learning.

Learning Byte   *When is the last time you went to class to learn a new skill outside of the work environment? If it has been greater than a month, does that mean that you haven't improved yourself in any way?*

Technological Considerations for On-Demand Learning

We live in a highly technological world. There have been several portions of this book that have discussed the technologic advances we are exposed to in our lives on a daily basis. In the world of learning and education, there is a separate technological revolution occurring. There are new content development and delivery tools that can deliver lessons over the web, on CDs, and to electronic books. There are tracking systems that can trace the electronic footsteps of users of online learning including web-based learning and CBTs. Complex network-based assessment engines allow learners to be directed in their learning with online quizzes and tests. Streaming video can be used to send synchronous and asynchronous lectures and presentations over the Internet. Chat rooms are used to hold virtual study groups. Internet pagers allow people to see when fellow learners are online to ask quick questions or to share interesting web pages. Business simulations are being used to fully simulate workflow from a user's desktop computer. There is a growing number of private firms that have learning technology that is so promising that many have recently gone public or have the potential to go public (e.g., Ask Jeeves and Ninth House). All of this use of technology is important and it will help hasten the migration away from classroom- and instructor-centered learning. But, is technology the panacea for all that ails learning? No… not by itself; however, technology can be a tremendous enabler of learning, if used appropriately.

This chapter provides insights on many of the things you need to consider if you want to use and deploy technologically enabled learning solutions that facilitate learning in your organization.
(Note: Not all organizations are large enough to have training departments or IT departments, or other support departments to use or implement all of the ideas that follow.)

In fact, many of you might be the company HR representative, trainer, and IT person rolled into one. Regardless of your organization's size, consider the points presented so that you will have an easier transition with the use of technology as your organization grows.

Technological Assessment

One of the first things you need to do when you are considering launching a technology-enabled learning solution across the enterprise is to ask yourself… "Why am I considering using technology to implement this learning intervention?" This is a very important question and one that you should be able to answer honestly and without hesitation. If you are using technology because you went to a web site and saw some new and cool solution demonstrated and you think that it would be cool to implement it where you work, then you should think twice about it. One of the deadliest mistakes people can make in the learning technology world is to use technology for the *whiz bang factor* (aka the *gee whiz factor*). Even if an account executive of a new learning technology company says that his or her company can build you something for next to nothing or free, you still need to know why you *need* to implement it. In my role at Dell Computer Corporation, I get several packages and advertising slicks, web sites, CDs, posters, demo software, etc., delivered in the mail every day. I also am inundated with phone calls, voice mail, and email from companies and individuals who claim to have the latest and hottest learning gadgetry going. All of these people are hawking solutions, and I don't hold that against them, because it's what they do. The point I am trying to make is that it is imperative that you have an actual business problem to solve with this technology rather than throwing solutions at *nonproblems*. I call these "solutions looking for problems" and when you start with a solution and try to match it with a problem the two never quite match. Now if the answer to the above question is, "I've got a business problem that is related to the high cost of training field-based personnel locally, and I need to find a solution to minimize those costs," then you are on the right track. You can actually build a functional requirements specification (FRS) based on the problem and farm this out to a group of solution vendors linked with specific acceptance criteria to make a better decision and get a better solution for the problem. (There is a template for an FRS in the Resource section of this book.) Vendors absolutely start to salivate when you tell them you need a solution and you haven't designed the functional requirements necessary for the solution. This allows the vendor to tell you what you need and it will gravitate around a solution the company already offers. The key is to *start with a problem...* not the solution.

Another issue to consider when you and your team are debating whether or not to use a technology-enabled learning solution is to try to take the pulse of the organization for the technology you are considering using. If you have never issued digitized video on CDs to your client groups it is important that you assess their readiness for this type of solution. Will learners use this kind of self-directed learning tool? Are there marketing and or open house sessions that can be used to showcase samples of the new tool prior to a wide release? Will the new technology be accessible to your target audience? That is, do they have the necessary hardware, software, and infrastructure to use the training? How descriptive do you need to be in the instructions for the new CD? How are you going to ensure that the CD is as easy to load and install as possible? Who will pay for the development, delivery, and ongoing maintenance of the solution? How long is the shelf-life of the product? How will the product be kept evergreen? Is the product meant to be disposable? Are there security issues (e.g., proprietary content on the CDs) that might prevent the tool's use? You've got to ask many questions (and answer them) before you even consider using technology as the basis of the solution.

Infrastructure Assessment

Once you are sure that you are building a technology-enabled learning solution for the right reasons, you must also survey the technology infrastructure in your work environment. You need to answer the following questions.

Do you have an Intranet?

This is a very basic but important question to ask. If you don't have an Intranet, then might you be able to recommend to the company leadership a learning web site or community as a central focus of a new Intranet?

What limitations are there for content, site size, and media types?

Each Intranet typically has some basic guidelines that are in place regarding content types, graphics sizes, and media types that can be used (e.g., streaming video, audio, animated web sites, etc.). The larger and more complex the Intranet, the more controls and guidelines there will be to help ensure consistency and data integrity. Consider a large corporate web site that has 50,000 web pages on it. Imagine the chaos and frustration of a person surfing such a large web site where each page has its own look, feel, and navigation strategy. The individual in this case has to learn how to navigate each new page. There are no friendly landmarks and no sure way to get back where you started. Even if you have a small Intranet, it is wise to incorporate standards so that as the Intranet grows there is some consistency throughout the site. It is also important to know what media types are allowable over corporate Intranets as well. If you want to send video clips over the Intranet, it is best to have these sitting on a dedicated video server (or set of servers) to ensure that the clips don't take a long time to download at the individual's desktop. Not all organizations allow the use of all media types over Intranets so it is important that you determine what you can and can't use.

Who can add and maintain content on the web servers?

This is a very important question that you must be able to answer. There are probably a group of people designated as web masters and/or administrators where you work. Smaller companies may have one individual who handles all aspects of the web including configuring web servers, building site directories, checking links, running web metrics reports, etc. If you want to be able to add information or if you want to be able to edit content on your learning web site, then you must have access and authority to do so as well as Hyper Text Markup Language (HTML) scripting knowledge. You need to also determine if contractors or vendors can access your site for new site development and also for web maintenance. I recommend that you have at least one other person beside yourself who can create and maintain web sites for you. I also recommend that you identify a content owner and a web person as a contact on each page that you publish. This is important because if a person browsing the web site notices a problem in the web site with content, he or she can contact the content owner to provide updated content to the web master to upload to the web server. This helps to keep the site fresh. I think there is nothing more frustrating than trying to track down the owner of a web page to get clarification on content. To minimize this aggravation, let people know who the owner is on each page. It might also be wise to consider *freshness dating* your web pages.

There is code that can be written into pages that will prevent them from being displayed on a given date. This will help ensure that out-of-date content is not the majority of what is on learning web sites.

What types of software and hardware are supported by your IT group?

You need to know specifically the allowable software that can be developed, supported, and maintained on your local networks and web servers. If you decide to try to bring a hardware or software type that is not supported by your IT organization you may have a hard time getting the system into production in your environment. It is imperative in large organizations and highly recommended in smaller organizations that any applications you develop and any hardware you purchase can be put into production. Production systems and software are typically supported by IT organizations. This may also involve use of a staging and developmental server. This way, if the production system crashes, the IT organization can quickly bring the application back up from the staging server copy of the application. This is important to remember. If you bring a new software or other application inside your firewall that is not supported by your IT group, you will inevitably spend extra money hiring full-time or contract help to provide ongoing maintenance and system upgrade support. Finally, when you bring in nonsupported software or hardware into your IT fold, you won't gain any IT fans quickly. Your IT department can save you if you have the right relationship established with them. The key in all of this is to work with your IT group to understand the standards and limitations for your specific network environment.

What is the bandwidth of your internal network?

It is important to get an understanding of the robustness of your internal network. There could be limitations around the types of applications you want to use that are related to the bandwidth of your local network. If you want to stream video, you will probably need to consider a dedicated video server (or bank of servers) to support this kind of application. Work with your IT department to identify strategies to minimize the space and speed requirements of learning applications you want to develop.

Can people access the internal network remotely?

The ability for people to access the internal network and/or the Intranet remotely is an important thing to know. If people can access the site remotely it allows you to create learning strategies that can include logging in from home or the field. Remote access is also important for you and other people who may need to do system maintenance on existing applications. You must also consider the access speed. Is 28.8 Kbps the maximum remote people can obtain? If so, it is going to affect the types of solutions you are going to create for remote personnel. You should consider another factor about modem speeds. A 56Kbps modem only operates at 56Kbps in ideal conditions. You might not always be connected at the optimum speed for your modem. New broadband technologies such as digital subscriber lines (DSL) and cable modems enable remote link speeds ten or more times faster. However, even with a high-speed remote link, there are other considerations such as security that may prevent remote operation. Use of encryption protocols such as Point to Point Tunneling Protocol (PPTP) and Layer 2 Tunneling Protocol (L2TP) can make remote links secure.

What browser(s) does your organization use?

You need to know the type of browser your organization uses because each browser has some limitations and coding that are specific to the individual browser. For example, some of the HTML extensions on codes that are specific to Microsoft Internet Explorer™ are not necessarily recognized by other browsers such as Netscape Communicator™. If you can control your environment, i.e., all users are in your department, you can develop for a specific browser type and version, using HTML extensions, etc. If you don't have control over your users' browser, e.g., you have users in many locations or from different organizations, it's better to develop strict standards that any supported browser can use. Of course, you should test your site on all variations of browser platform that personnel might use.

Can you use commonly deployed plug-ins?

Various organizations have different requirements for the use of plug-ins inside the network. Plug-ins are special mini-applications that give web-based applications increased functionality. One good example of this is Shockwave™ from Macromedia. This plug-in allows animation in web-based applications. However, plug-ins are not always globally acceptable to your IT department. Some plug-ins wreak havoc on IT systems and cause additional work and support for IT departments to handle. Check with your IT department to determine what plug-ins are are already part of your standards or are acceptable to use and/or deploy across your enterprise. Plug-ins can be very effective in providing additional functionality to static web sites.

Design Considerations

Now that we've discussed some of the infrastructure and other related technology questions, let's take a look at some design and content considerations for technology-enabled on-demand learning. Consider the following questions.

What types of information can be put on the Intranet?

This may seem like a silly question to ask, but it is a key question you will need to ask and answer. Are you allowed to post sensitive and/or confidential information on your web site? Who has to authorize content that gets posted? If there is no special corporate security team or other organization that must authorize content posting, you can streamline your posting time. You must also determine how long the information will be valid so that you can freshness date the content (or use database-driven web sites to assist with this). If you are going to include monthly data, incorporate a system that allows a person or team to update this information quickly. You'll also need to identify content owners for each page to facilitate keeping the content current. Another important point to determine is whether or not your organization is allowed to tap into pre-existing external web sites. If you can tap into the many Internet resources out there, you can save a tremendous amount of time in the design and development of new on-demand learning solutions. However, not all companies allow this process to happen. Furthermore, you need to regularly link-check your web site to ensure these links remain valid.

What limitations are imposed on graphics? What size limitations are there?

Determine the preferred web format for graphics. Usually it is .gif for graphics and .jpg for photos because of the reduced file size and browser compatibility. As with content, some graphics can become outdated and useless, so you need to identify ways to tag these graphics so that they can be refreshed as needed. Keep in mind that graphics are more complex, time consuming, and expensive to update, so try to keep the graphic data as long-lived as possible.

Who can check my learning site or tool for legal and/or security issues?
It is important that you develop a special and close relationship with IT, Legal, and Information Security (or Information Protection) in your organization. As was mentioned earlier, not all content can be readily distributed across the Intranet or other internal networks. These folks can help you determine what can be accessed, who can access it, and how it can be accessed. In addition to potential dissemination of sensitive materials outside your firewall, you may also need to be concerned about internal security. Some information may need to be restricted to certain internal audiences, either permanently or temporarily. For example, if you were tasked with developing a web-based training program to explain your company's quarterly results, this would likely be restricted information until the public announcement of the results. Using various security mechanisms, your IT group should be able to restrict access to named users or groups. Your legal department can help you identify potential legal issues around the content and learning opportunities you want to provide. For example, in companies that sell products and/or services, there are Federal Trade Commission laws on what can and can't be said about products that are sold. If you develop learning solutions that teach people to use the wrong sales pitch or mislead a customer, your organization could be held liable. Your IT organization can help you with a variety of techniques to help you lock down your site.

What restrictions, if any, are there on access to the Internet?
Related to this is the need to know what kind of access people can get to your internal web site. It is important to know this for several reasons. If you plan to let people access the learning network from outside of the firewall, then you need to ensure that this is allowable. Such a system is often called an Extranet. Your IT department will let you know how this can be done and what (if any) limitations this can cause. I recommend that you log in from several locations and from a variety of system types as close as possible to those that your end users will use to help ascertain system performance for external people. If system response time is slow, you might consider the use of distributed CDs or other technology to improve learning performance for remote personnel. Another reason this is important is for potential vendors and other outside resources that

might be helping you develop and/or maintain your web site. If they can't access the site, they will have to come to your site to do this type of work for you, which can make it more expensive.

Can outside vendors build web sites and/or custom CBT for you, or do you have to do it all in-house?

An important consideration is to determine whether or not you have the in-house core competence to build learning web sites and other online learning interventions. In many organizations, there is a sense that if internal personnel do not create solutions, then the subsequent product is not valuable. This can be true in some cases, however, I recommend that you outsource development appropriately to qualified internal or external consultants. Use your experience, learning solution design, and project management skills to create the best possible solution. Your value-added in projects like these is making the appropriate resource connections inside of your organization for the consultant you have hired. You can direct the consultant to the best source of IT, Legal, Procurement, and other types of information needed to complete the work.

One other advantage of outsourcing is the flexibility that it allows you and your team. If there are four people on your team and you don't outsource any work for the team, there will be a saturation point of projects that can be completed by your team. Managing vendors and consultants to help complete projects allows your team members to work on more projects than they could alone.

Where do you find qualified consultants?

One of the most challenging tasks before you when you try to outsource work in online learning solution development is finding qualified consultants. This is critical because selecting the wrong consultant(s) can cost you time, effort, opportunity costs, credibility, and quality.

Before we delve any further, I'd like you to consider a distinction I make between consultants and contractors. This is important because it can help you make decisions about who to choose to do work in certain situations. In my mind, a consultant is a highly qualified expert in a field(s) of interest. Consultants generally work on project-related work that has a specific start and end with clearly defined deliverables. Consultants also generally have more than one client that they service.

Consultants are not completely dependent on you or any other singular organization for their survival. Contractors work with one client over a specified period of time (and not necessarily on a specific project). Consultants who are relying on your organization for survival can cause many problems for you as time passes. They lose some of the entrepreneurial spirit that attracted them to you in the beginning. They can learn how to work the system to their advantage. And, they can hold your organization hostage by creating vendor dependence. You always want to have more than one person, team, or organization that can complete critical tasks, since in today's churning work environment and in this age of corporate free agency people can pick up and leave whenever they like.

So, it is important to identify and have appropriate cover for your jobs. Here are some places you can find online learning solution developers:

- Classified ads in local newspapers
- Web sites, including www.trainingnet.com, www.esourcecorp.com, and other local web sites
- College campus classifieds
- Technical schools
- Local chapters of organizations such as the International Society for Training and Performance (ISPI) and the American Society for Training and Development (ASTD)
- Word of mouth from other people in your organization
- Professional organizations in the subject matter field, e.g., IEEE for Electrical and Electronic Engineering

If you think you have found the right consultant, you might want to ask the following questions to get a sense of qualifications and fit:

- How long have you been in business?
- What other clients have you supported?
- What references can you supply? (It is important that you check these references.)
- What work samples or sites can I see or access?
- What are your rates?
- What kind of guarantee do you have on your work?
- How many people are in your organization?

- How will you ensure that I'll always have coverage for projects that you are working on for us?
- What support do you provide? (e.g., hours of operation, who fixes/pays for bugs discovered after installation, etc.)
- Have you ever done any work for this organization?
- What does a typical online learning solution development project entail?
- What are the major steps, and how would you proceed?
- How do you cost projects?
- Has your work won any awards in the industry?

This list of questions will help you get a sense of what the consultant will be able to do or not do for you in support of the project you need completed. Don't rush the decision on consultant choice. The right consultant can make all of the difference in the world, so it is worth exploring this appropriately to get the best match. It doesn't hurt to have a couple of alternative vendors at the ready either in case things don't work well with the primary vendor.

How much does it cost to have online on-demand learning solutions built?
There is a tremendous amount of variability in project cost. There are different costs for different media. The type of programming required can affect the cost. For example, static HTML programming is much less expensive than dynamic or database-driven active server page (ASP) development. Custom computer-based training (CBT) is more expensive than static web sites, too. Everything depends on the complexity of the programming, scarcity of developers, amount and complexity of content, scope of the work, and required completion time. When you work with a consultant, get a detailed statement of work, including timelines and costs per task. Use these if necessary to compare what similar vendors would charge for the work. Make your decision, come to agreement, and get rolling on the project.

What types of resources are commonly used to build a web site or CBT?
There are many people who will need to be involved in the development of a successful learning web site or CBT. Here is a list of folks that should be involved in the project:

- Project Sponsor
- Project Manager
- Instructional Designer
- Web Master and/or Developer
- Database Administrator (if the site or CBT is dynamic and database-driven)
- Graphic Artist
- Technical Writer/Editor
- Subject Matter Experts (SMEs)
- End Users (for usability studies)
- Extended Team Members (from Legal, IT, Procurement, Information Protection, etc.)

As you can see it takes more than one person to create a successful learning solution. Plan early and work with the core and extended team to create the best possible project.

Cost: high upfront but lower later

There is one other design consideration that is important, especially if you will need to make a business case to get the solution implemented. Technology-enabled learning solutions, generally, have higher upfront costs and lower recurring costs than comparative conventional solutions. However, they can have much greater impact to a much larger audience more quickly. Look at this scenario. Company A is going to create compliance training for its 750 managers on Preventing Sexual Harassment using a three-hour classroom session. Company B is going to create the same training using one-hour web-based learning for the same size target audience. It takes companies A and B eight weeks to get the solution created. Let's say for the sake of this scenario that the online solution cost $35,000 to design and ready for implementation, but the classroom only cost $25,000 to develop. At first glance, the classroom solution may look like the one to choose, however, let's look at the scenarios a little more closely. Now that the classroom is developed, with a maximum classroom size of 35 participants, how many classes have to be scheduled with expensive instructors to impact the entire audience? At least twenty-one classes will have to be scheduled, to get all of the managers trained on the same content. This could take several months. What are the costs associated with travel to and from the training room? What are the opportunity costs associated with 750 managers being out of their normal workplace for three plus hours? What happens when you add in cancellations, no-shows, and rescheduling? Many training organizations charge cost centers for no-shows and cancellations, so costs can really start to grow. Now, contrast this with the web-based learning solution. All 750 managers could access the learning in the first week if necessary, because it is not dependent on instructors, classrooms, travel time, etc. A maximum impact can be achieved across the organization quickly. Less time is spent away from the job. And the solution remains available with little or no recurring costs for new employees, which is an important consideration in fast-growing companies. The managers can access the learning quickly when they want to and later on as a reference. So, sometimes the slightly additional cost upfront more than pays for itself in the end.

The business need for learning can evaporate if too much time elapses as well. If it takes too long to get a solution out to the enterprise, the original business need that predicated the training originally can disappear. This is another consideration when deciding on the type of solution to implement.

When Not to Use Technology-Based Solutions

There are times when you definitely don't want to use technology-enabled solutions. Do not use technology-enabled solutions when:

- A sound nontechnology enabled solution is available
- Technology is being used for the sake of technology (aka the gee whiz factor)
- The technology-enabled solution will be more difficult to use than a similar conventional solution
- The Return on Investment (ROI) doesn't exist when using it
- The infrastructure is not in place to support it
- It will not be able to be maintained
- It will not be able to solve an actual business problem
- The organizational culture is not ready to embrace it
- The technology-enabled solution is not scalable

The use of technology by itself to enable learning is not a learning panacea. Technology is just one enabler in a whole series of enablers that must exist for learning, retention, and transfer to occur.

Administering On-Demand Solutions

Another important aspect of on-demand learning solutions is administering them. There are many considerations when implementing an on-demand learning solution. How will participants be able to access the on-demand learning solution? Will participants get credit for their learning? If so, how much? Will participants be able to self-register? Will there be a course catalog? If so, who will write it? Who will ensure that it is current? Will participants be charged for on-demand learning solutions? If so, what does the pricing model look like? How will money actually be transferred from cost center to cost center? Who will evaluate the quality of on-demand learning solutions? Who will make recommendations to edit or delete on-demand learning solutions? How many people will be needed to administer on-demand learning solutions? Strategically, in what direction is the learning organization headed? Will there be more or less on-demand learning solutions?

All of these things must be considered. One way that some of these questions can be answered is with the use of tracking systems.

Tracking On-Demand Learning Solutions

There is a saying, "If you can't measure it, you can't manage it." This is very true in the case of on-demand learning solutions. If you are managing development and delivery of on-demand learning solutions, you must be able to track usage. Upper management will want to know what people are using, what they are spending on alternative learning methods, how often employees are using on-demand learning solutions, and so forth. If you can't track this kind of information you will find it hard to accurately report on it. That's where a tracking/administration system is imperative.

There are many tracking and administration systems available. It is important that you get the system that is appropriate for your organization's needs. Tracking systems are generally divided into two types (using one of two metaphoric models). One type is based on the traditional centralized or academic learning model. Resources and classes are managed using these systems. Their prime focus is to get instructors, participants, materials, and classrooms synchronized so that people can get the training they want. They are in essence event managers. The second model that is used is CBT or online learning tracking. These systems were designed from the beginning to track specific information

Technological Considerations for On-Demand Learning

associated with the use of on-demand online learning solutions. There are some solutions that can track both classroom and online learning solutions, but most don't. There is a list of some companies that provide tracking systems in the Resource section of this book.

How should you and your organization make the determination for the type of online tracking system you are going to use? I recommend the following:

1. *Identify the functional requirements you have for the tracking system in your organization.* What do you need the tracking system to be able to do? What are you going to track, i.e., what data and information do stakeholders want to see? How will it be administered? What IT requirements have to be met to bring the solution into your enterprise? What is the budget for the solution? What functionality must you have? What functionality is nice to have? Will you use reporting in the system or report using a company-resident reporting system? What systems will the tracking system need to interface with?

2. *Create a matrix that has all of your criteria on it.* This can be used as part of a Request for Proposal (RFP) to get the best possible fit for your needs. You will want to work with your procurement department to ensure that you are completing the RFP process appropriately. Create a scoring sheet for key requirements, weighted by importance. This helps ensure the evaluation is objective, not subjective.

3. *Identify vendors who have applications you need.* You can send out the RFP to the list of vendors.

4. *Review the proposal responses.* Based on selection criteria you have created, and using your scoring sheet, cull the list of proposals (vendors) down to three or four finalists that can meet all of your key requests. Rate/rank the proposals using your scoring sheet.

5. *Notify the finalists.* Request on-site visits and demonstrations of the product for your team. If possible, speak with reference accounts for the vendors. Ask to speak with accounts with positive and negative implementations to get a sense of what happened.

6. *Make final decision.* Based on team input, choose the application and implement it in your organization.

Once the tracking system is in place, it will be much easier to track and administer online learning solutions. When you can measure the use of online learning solutions you will be able to manage them.

You will also need to determine the types of metrics you will use to measure the effectiveness of the solution you are bringing to bear. Here are some things you might consider measuring:

- Online courses taken per person and per business unit
- Percent of target audience completing the training
- Average time spent in each online learning solution
- Amount of money charged for online learning
- Ways people navigate through online learning
- Solution effectiveness
- Knowledge-based or performance-based evaluations
- Return on Investment data, if possible

All of these things are important to consider when developing metrics for online learning solutions.

Summary

There are many considerations for those who want to explore the use of technology-based learning solutions across their enterprises. You must consider your end-goal for the technology-enabled solution, the infrastructure you have, how to get the solutions developed, who can develop them for you, how you will maintain them, and how you will track them once in place. These are not things to consider lightly, since thorough planning and adherence to functional requirements will facilitate implementation of a more powerful solution.

In the next chapter, I share some industry best practices in on-demand learning.

Learning Byte   *Does your learning solution have to be in place for the ages? If not, don't build it for the ages. It can really change the way you design learning solutions in a positive way.*

On-Demand Learning Best Practices (Employee and Customer Examples)

This section of the book provides examples of on-demand learning in use today which you can use to help create your own self-directed learning solutions. There are conventional (minimal or no technology involved), hybrid (some technology involved), and high-tech (greatly enhanced with technology) examples. Most of the examples are geared towards employees, but some are focused on learning for the customer (a group that is getting more and more attention across the United States and abroad.)

One other thing is important for you to note. I've tried to include a business problem in all of the solutions that I present. Some of the solutions featured are so new that some companies were sensitive about releasing client names and product uses. However, some of the products are so compelling that I've decided to feature them without explicit business cases.

Conventional Examples

Not all learning solutions have to be high-tech or Internet-based to be effective. To the contrary, some of the most powerful learning solutions I've seen are simple yet powerful. They provide access to key information, knowledge, or skills just as (or just before) the end user needs it.

Badge Aids

At Dell, one of the best examples of a low-tech on-demand learning tool are things I call badge aids. We create separate badges for various kinds of information that people need to have on hand all of the time. For instance, for Dell Learning, I have the entire Dell Learning corporate organization contact information on a two-sided card that fits right behind my regular badge. The badge hangs on my belt. If I need to get the extension of one of my fellow Dell Learning associates, I can quickly look at the card and get the five-digit extension for the call. I've also got some for benefits, a vacation calendar, acronyms, and other useful information.

As a part of our new hire orientation, a series of badge aids are sent to the prospective employees with other information that will help them to have information they need right at their finger tips. The employee can select those badge aids he or she feels will help the most on the job. Most companies and organizations use security badges in one form or another, and this is a great way to put key information, process steps, contact information, etc., at the fingertips of those people who need them.

There are badge laminating machines and hole punches that can be used to create the badge aids. It is a good idea to create a template for these so new ones can be created quickly as the need arises. Keep a template file in a word processor or graphics program that allows the creator to build these on the fly. Alternatively, these can be mass-produced at most commercial print shops.

Computer Flipcards

The real estate near and around our computer monitors is valuable. Many knowledge workers spend many hours a day using their computers to complete the many tasks associated with their jobs. A Company called Left Coast Interactive, in Mill Valley, California, has figured this out and developed a creative job aid for a variety of end uses. These laminated dye-cut cards attach to one side of your monitor with special hinges.

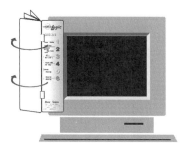

These computer flipcards keep essential information close at hand, such as software codes and instructions, procedures and guidelines, checklists and tables, product information, calendars and schedules, customer service information, Uniform Resource Locators (URLs) and email addresses, and phone and fax numbers. These cards can be used for customer service representatives, sales representatives, order processors, collections personnel, managers, and any other employees in need of quick access to memory joggers for the job.

The flipcards are a low-cost job aid that provides benefits including quicker integration of new systems, reduced recurrent coding errors, lower number of technical support calls, minimized need for training, and increased independent work, consistent performance, and cross training. The cards can be completely customized with any organization's content. Left Coast Interactive also has a variety of stock cards such as Office 97™, Lotus Notes™, Office 2000™, Outlook98™, Word Perfect™, and Windows NT™.

Computer Monitor Frames

Because many people spend a large amount of time in front of their desktop computers, there are several companies that sell generic and customized computer monitor frames. These frames (normally a thin laminated piece of cardboard) fit perfectly around the frame of the monitor. The monitor frame can be written on with a grease pencil for personalized notes, or can come with customized notes or procedures or software shortcuts.

Einstein Brothers Bagel Sandwich Making Aids

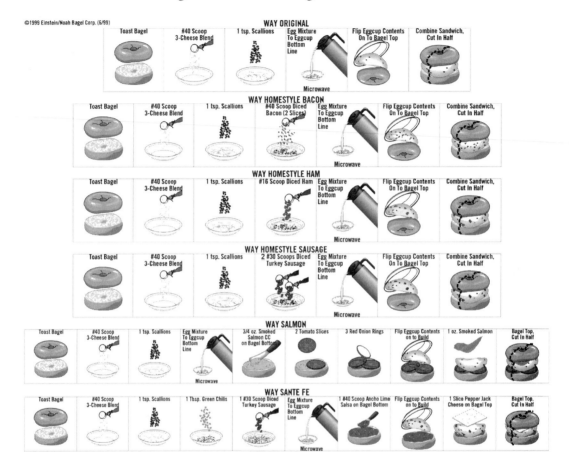

©1999 Einstein/Noah Bagel Corp. (6/99)

I walked into a local Einstein Brothers Bagel store one day to get some lunch and discovered a terrific example of on-demand learning in use by their staff. The employees were using one-page laminated sandwich templates. They are pictographic, four-color, reusable, and relatively inexpensive. They show graphically how an employee should build the sandwiches that the store serves. It helps ensure consistent look and consistent quality of sandwiches and other products that the Einstein Brothers crew creates.

HRD Press Pocket Manager Series and Assessment Tools

HRD Press (www.hrdpress.com or 1-800-822-2801) is a publishing house from Amherst, Massachusetts, that targets the Human Resources function publishing arena. They publish and distribute courseware, books, assessment instruments, job aids, and other tools the professional HR person will find beneficial.

One interesting example of on-demand learning tools they offer is *The Manager's Pocket Guide*™ series of books. These books literally fit in your pocket. They are easy to read yet well-written and insightful. They cover a broad range of topics including:

- Conflict Resolution
- Effective Mentoring
- Performance Management
- Team Sponsorship
- Creativity
- Effective Meetings
- Employee Relations
- Documenting Employee Performance
- And many others

The books are laden with checklists, guidance, and information on a variety of subject areas critical to the manager.

Another set of useful on-demand learning tools from HRD Press is their assessment tools. One great way to enable (and streamline) the self-directed learning process is to assess the current level of the learner. HRD Press has a series of inventories and assessments that allow individuals to self-assess where they are in a variety of topical areas including:

- Management Competencies
- 360° Leadership Assessment and Development Tool
- Performance Skills Leader Assessment
- Adult Mentoring Inventory
- Insight Inventory®
- Learning Style Questionnaire
- And many others

If the learner can identify what areas they are competent in and what areas they need to develop more, they can streamline their learning processes. This enables the learner to focus on those areas they need to and minimizes redundant work in the learning process. If you don't know where you are, it is hard to get where you want to go.

The InternetMap Company

The Internet has become as engrained in our culture and in our workspaces as the telephone, voice mail, and the fax machine. Many companies are embracing the just-in-time business information and support that the Internet provides. So what's the problem? The problem is that many people who haven't used the Internet can have real doubts and misgivings about exploring the Internet. They don't know what a Uniform Resource Locator (URL) is or what an Internet Service Provider (ISP) is. Some folks are baffled by the dots and forward slashes and silly addresses that the Internet uses to route people to servers on its extensive global network. Some people know these things, but just want some more information on how the Internet works with key sites they can surf and user-friendly search engines. Enter Clay Curtis.

Clay Curtis, an artist and entrepreneur, embarked upon his personal discovery of the Internet…and soon became lost in a vast sea of dry text and listless diagrams. What he wanted was a quick reference, a visual guide to walk him through the basics. What he did not want was to be forced to read a half-dozen textbooks in order to efficiently make use of a tool that many schoolchildren take for granted. A quick search of local computer centers and bookstores revealed a complete lack of any sort of basic visual reference. In the rush to provide the latest cutting edge, technological advancements in a booming industry the industry leaders had forgotten about the basics. As a self-employed business owner, Clay Curtis realized he was on his own: as an artist and an entrepreneur he quickly made the decision to create what others had overlooked.

The Internet Map Company was created to "map" the Internet — to create a visual reference that would help beginning Internet users understand and make better use of the Internet. Several early prototypes used flowcharts, schematics, and the sort of techno-babble drawings you might expect of a fairly technical concept before it finally occurred to Clay that the people who need this visual reference are not technical people nor do they need a technical explanation. They are typically "the average person," whose only need in understanding this sometimes confusing and intimidating concept is that it be presented in a familiar and nonintimidating manner. For most people, the Internet is visually unfathomable — they just can't *see* it. Ask someone to visually describe the Internet and they will usually try to tell you how various parts of it work, never what it looks like. This makes teaching the concept of "what the Internet is" that much more difficult.

The idea behind The Internet Map is to use a familiar analogy to describe the indescribable — to compare the Internet to something that the average person finds comfortably familiar. It is a proven fact that many people are visual learners and will generally grasp a concept quicker and more thoroughly if they can visualize the concept, particularly if it is put into a familiar form. The use of thematic approaches with adult learners is a proven accelerated learning technique that draws upon the experiences of people and helps puts a context around nondiscreet theories and knowledge.

The Internet Map uses the familiar analogy of going to an airport and travelling by air to describe the process of getting online and exploring the Internet. Clay has broken down the Internet into five major task-related areas: Email, Chat, Newsgroups, File Transfer Protocol (FTP), and The Web and compared them to familiar facets of air travel. In addition, most of the key components used in Internet "travel," such as Service Providers, Web Browsers and Modems, are explained by comparing them with the key components of air travel such as security gates, airlines, and planes. The text is written in everyday language and where it was necessary to introduce unfamiliar terms (such as HTML, link, protocol, etc.) Clay has included an accompanying list of Key Terms with clearly worded definitions. An example of the information presented on the poster can be seen at theinternetmap.com.

As part of a market test, in 1999 The Internet Map was mailed to over 1,100 schools in eight North Texas counties. Clay and his company have received numerous calls and letters of thanks and support: The Internet Map poster has proven to be a fun yet effective Internet-education tool from elementary through the college level.

The Internet Map is also an excellent marketing tool for companies looking for a way to promote their presence on the Internet. By helping their potential customers better understand the Internet they are helping future customers make better use of a tool that will be used to browse through product lines, get technical support or customer service, view promotional information, locate offices or key personnel, and ultimately, conduct commercial transactions. The Internet Map Company can also extend the analogy by "mapping out" corporate web sites to further the customer's ability to make use of these sites.

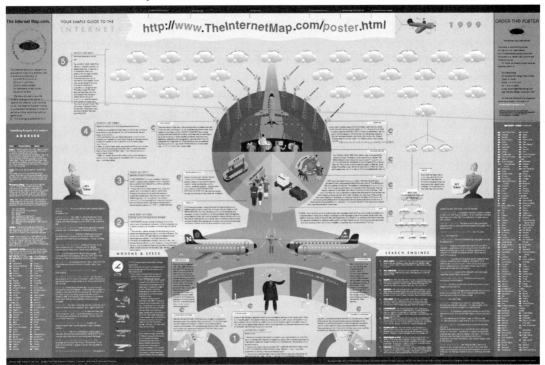

Additionally, The Internet Map can graphically represent corporate Intranets for companies wanting to improve employee awareness and ability in using internal, corporate Internet tools. For example, say your organization is going to implement a new enterprise-wide learning intervention on a new web-based tool. When the web-based learning is advertised or marketed, The Internet Map can be customized with specific Intranet addresses and provide a vivid reminder of the initiative to all employees.

The Internet Map is available to the public in a 24"x 36" high-quality, glossy, finished poster and is available to corporate clients in either the poster format or broken down by section and presented in a 5"x 8" saddle-stitched booklet.

Southwest Airlines In-Flight Service Reminders and Checklists

Fun Favors

CHANGE ☐ 165 KIT ☐ WINE KIT ☐ BEER KIT left back right (circle one)

EXTRA ☐ PEANUTS ☐ RAISINS ☐ LEMONS/LIMES

CABIN CLEAN-UP BAG ☐ BIOHAZARD BAGS ☐ SOLIDIFIER ☐ PPE KITS ☐ INVESTIGATION FORMS ☐ TRACKING LABELS ☐ SYRINGE TUBES

LAV ATTENTION ☐ EMPTY TRASH ☐ PAPER GOODS ☐ FEM SUPPLIES

☐ EMPTY ALUMINUM RECYCLE BIN	☐ DRINK ORDER PADS
☐ LIQUOR ENVELOPES	☐ SANICOM WIPES
☐ ENTERTAINMENT KIT	☐ BIOHAZARD CLEAN-UP KIT (formerly Vital 1)
☐ LATEX GLOVES	☐ MEDICAL SUPPLIES (SPECIFY)
☐ TRASH BAGS (REGULAR / RECYCLE)	☐ DISINFECTANT
☐ CLEAR PLASTIC LIDS	☐ AIR FRESHENER
☐ COFFEE LIDS	☐ LIQUID SOAP
☐ STRAWS	☐ TAKE EXTRA SNACKS
☐ REPLACE SNACK BASKET	☐ REPLACE SERVING TRAY
☐ OTHER _____	

SEQUENCE OF SERVICE GUIDELINES
(Flight Times Approximate)

90 Minutes or Less	90 Minutes to 3 Hours designated **S**	3 Hours to 5 Hours designated **SP**	5 Hours or More designated **LH** Depart before 1000	5 Hours or More designated **LH** Depart after 1000
AFTER TAKEOFF				
Depart before 0930	Beverages Peanuts (Raisins as an alternative)	Depart before 1000	Beverages Sweet Snack Pick up - Seconds	Beverages Peanuts (Raisins as an alternative)
Coffee/Juice Pick up - Seconds	Snack	Beverages Sweet Snack Pick up - Seconds	**MID FLIGHT**	Snack Pack Pick up - Seconds
	Pick up - Seconds	Depart after 1000	Approx. 2.5 hours before landing	**MID FLIGHT**
Depart after 0930		Beverages Peanuts (Raisins as an alternative) Snack Pick up - Seconds	Coffee/Water	Approx. 2.5 hours before landing
Beverages Peanuts (Raisins as an alternative)			Approx. 2 hours before landing	Coffee/Water
Pick up - Seconds		**MID FLIGHT**	Beverages Peanuts (Raisins as an alternative) Snack Pack Pick up - Seconds	Approx. 2 hours before landing
		Approx. 2 hours before landing		Beverages Peanuts (Raisins as an alternative) Salty Snack Pick up - Seconds
		Coffee/Water Beverages Pick up - Seconds	**BEFORE LANDING**	**BEFORE LANDING**
		BEFORE LANDING	Approx. 30 minutes	Approx. 30 minutes
		Approx. 30 minutes	Single wrapped cookie	Single wrapped cookie
		Single wrapped cookie		

PV-09A (Rev. 4/99)

I was recently on a Southwest Airlines flight from Baltimore/
Washington to Austin, Texas. The flight was completely full. After we
had taken off, the flight attendants went row by row, person by person, to
determine what drinks people wanted. I was curious about how they
always got the drink orders right. I noticed them writing things down on
a pad. I asked the flight attendant if I could have one and she graciously
complied (the flight attendants are so nice on Southwest). It is one of the
most interesting examples of a conventional on-demand learning aid I've
seen.

On one side (see the picture) is a "Fun Favors" list. This is where flight attendants can put requests in for things like cocktail mixes, cleaning supplies, more peanuts or snacks, etc. The reason it is called a Fun Favors list is because an underlying philosophy and value of Southwest Airlines is to have fun! It's used as a just-in-time inventory tool for the ground crew to use during the plane's turnaround. It provides a guideline for flight crews to use to help ensure quality in-flight service and appropriate restocking of supplies. Southwest jets are normally only on the ground between flights for twenty minutes, so knowing exactly what needs to be replaced is a huge timesaver for the ground crews.

Below the Fun Favors list is a great job aid for in-flight snack and beverage service. It is broken down into categories for flight length, time of flight, etc., that let the flight attendant know when to serve beverages and/or snacks to the passengers, when to replenish snacks, and so forth. This is extremely useful for new flight attendants who are getting used to the schedule.

The other side of the form has the rows listed on the airplane. Each row number has a column for the seats as well. When the flight attendant goes through the aisle and asks what the preferred drink is, he or she annotates the drink (with acronyms) on the sheet. Now when the flight attendant goes back to the galley, getting the right drinks for the passengers is a snap. The flight attendant is able to learn the right refreshments to disburse at the right time, so this is another great example of on-demand learning.

Hybrid Examples

How The Limited, Inc., Accessorizes Its Instructor-Led Learning for Maximum Impact

The Limited was founded by Leslie H. Wexner on Aug. 10, 1963, beginning with one store located at Columbus, Ohio's Kingsdale Center. The Limited has since grown to 5,633 stores and 13 retail businesses. Included under the LTD stock symbol are Limited Stores, Express, Lerner

New York, Lane Bryant, Henri Bendel, Structure, Limited Too and Galyan's Trading Company. The Limited also owns 83 percent of the shares of Intimate Brands, Inc., IBI, which consists of Bath & Body Works, Victoria's Secret Stores and Victoria's Secret Catalogue, and an 84 percent interest in Abercrombie & Fitch, ANF. For more corporate information go to **www.limited.com** on the Internet.

One of the key reasons for the success of the organization lies in its outstanding training and development which is under the leadership of Beth Thomas. She shared some of the reasons for her organization's success and some of the practices her team employs in the learning and development field. Her client list is varied as you can see from the paragraph above, and so are the learning styles and solutions that she must employ to meet the training needs of her client bases. "A challenge in today's learning industry is being able to develop a *Just in Time (JIT) Learning* environment in a convenient, relevant and interactive fashion. What is the right solution to this challenge? I believe there is not simply one standard solution for everyone, rather there are multiple solutions that vary depending on your type of business, your audience and the location of your audience."

Beth stresses the importance of starting with a business problem and ensuring the proposed solution meets the needs of the end users. "For all Limited, Inc., businesses, we strive to bring this type of learning to each of our Headquarter associates. The key to developing your learning strategy is to ensure that whatever JIT learning solution(s) you choose, you pilot the solution in your business prior to making the investment. It has to be right for your business. Just because CBT / Online Learning is one of the fastest and most convenient ways to deploy training, it may not be the right answer for your company." Work with your business. Analyze the needs of your audience and create the best possible solution.

Training at The Limited, Inc., is customized to support technologies and business processes. Most training is instructor-led and because of the nature of the learning and skills that are to be transferred this is very appropriate for the people Beth's organization supports. There are other forms of learning at The Limited, Inc., and in alignment with her industry, Beth calls many of these alternative learning methods *accessories*. Beth says, "It is crucial you offer other learning avenues or accessories to your instructor-led training (ILT) programs, such as Online Learning. The largest benefit of Online Learning is that you have the ability to (1) provide training to those associates located in geographically disbursed communities and (2) offer classes as a source of pre-requisite training for ILT and (3) most importantly provide a means of immediate support as they need it."

I asked Beth to provide some examples of learning accessories that The Limited, Inc., uses. Here are some of the Intranet-based samples she offered:

- Tips, tricks, and hints on all of our top business critical applications & MS products
- "Lingo Look-up" where you can seek and find the meaning of any business specific retail terminology
- A recommended technology career path for our business critical roles
- Online skills assessment to help determine what classes an associate needs
- Training manuals and student files
- Videos / books / online library that includes links to important training/learning sites
- Business or industry specific information, e.g., Y2000 page — What is it? How does it affect me?
- Pages of success stories sent from our customers to explain how our training has made them more effective in their role and to share "best practices" regarding our technologies and processes
- Online review of our class curriculum, easy online registration, and review of the classes you have taken year-to-date

In addition to the Intranet-based content, tools, and activities there are other available services such as:

- Technical online learning available for our IT community
- ON-DEMAND — an interactive Electronic Performance Support System for all Microsoft Desktop applications
- Quick reference cards for all of our desktop and customized applications
- One on One Training (even "home" training for executives on nights and weekends!)
- Sneaker-Based Training or Learning Labs – where the training specialist works with an associate one-on-one, at the associate's

desk with his or her own work (Sneaker-based because a training specialist is going directly to people's desks to provide coaching and learning services.)

- Brown Bag lunches – short subject matter classes, such as "How to Buy a PC for Home" or "Getting Hooked to the Intranet"
- Training HOTLINE so associates can inquire about our classes and services and schedule a private appointment with our trainers. The Training HOTLINE also will assist associates in finding classes we do not offer internally, "If we don't train it, we'll find it!"
- In the near future The Limited, Inc., will offer online learning for all Microsoft™ Desktop applications

Beth Thomas and The Limited, Inc., learning organization have leveraged the variety of learning styles to create variety in the learning solutions offered. "Adults learn in many different ways. Some of us like to learn on our own or some of us may need more facilitated guidance. This is an analysis that is very important to do for your environment prior to making any decisions or investments. I would rather invest a little more to make our learning programs effective and realize a high Return on Investment then going after a 'cheaper' or more technically advanced solution that has little or no Return on Investment."

Beth can back up her philosophies with solid data. "The Limited is getting a big return on its investment. Three years ago, Thomas trained 50 people per month, with a cancellation/no-show rate of 35 percent to 50 percent. Today she and her 12-person team train as many as 1,000 people per month, with a cancellation/no-show rate of less than 5 percent. The sessions vary widely — from an entry-level class on the basics of retail to a 60-hour course on how to use business-critical applications to make better decisions" (Imperato, p. 46).

In summary, there are a variety of solutions that will help enable on-demand learning based on the learning styles of the participants and the business problems the learning organization is trying to help solve. Beth Thomas and The Limited, Inc., have determined how to accessorize their learning opportunities for maximum effectiveness and access.

CDs for Product and Sales Training

Sales representatives often do not possess sufficient product knowledge to make effective sales presentations for a variety of reasons including: lack of time, dislike of reading, believing their "relationship" will get the order, laziness, etc. But it's usually because they have a large number of products to sell. This happens with manufacturers that have their own sales force, manufacturers who employ "Independent Manufacturers Agents," and with independent distributors.

Salespeople need more convenient ways of learning and reviewing the features, functions, benefits, and applications of the specific products they are responsible for selling. Sales reps, especially those who spend a lot of time in the car, ultimate spend fifteen to twenty hours per week in drive time and except for the use of the phone, the time is usually unproductive. The three-ring binders and print collateral that are furnished to reps are needed for reference and for those who will read the literature. However, having the ability to additionally review, or learn for the first time, product information right before making a presentation (on-demand) is the most effective way to help ensure that the sales presentation includes the unique, differentiating selling points that help reps address objections and close sales.

Lack of effective sales training and support causes loss of sales, commission, revenues, margin, market share, sales force motivation, and potentially jobs! So, how do you help support the learning of a widely distributed network of field sales representatives and account managers? There are a variety of ways one can do this including custom CBT, job aids, books, videotapes, etc. Dan Bryant of Companion Audio Communications, Inc., has been producing a series of products that get critical product information to target audiences in their cars, in their portable computers, and any other place they can use CDs or cassettes. Companion Audio products also incorporate other learning methods such as visual imagery, repetition, review, numbering, acronyms, and "information-chunking."

Dan states: "We're called upon, usually by manufacturers, to create a variety of audio-based communications to be listened to in the car by their first line sales representatives. Sometimes the audio program is designed for other level of reps...say the manufacturer has 100 reps who are direct employees...who manage an independent rep force of another 100....who call on distributors (who also have reps). The audio can be designed for a single level of reps...or more generically for all to hear."

Content has included company news, promotion information, new technology updates, incentive program guidelines, benefits packages, and product specific audio programs that go with the Salesmaker Acceleration System. The system includes an audio program (audio tape or CD), a pocket-sized laminated TIPS card (TIPS stands for Technical

Information for Power Selling), and also three postcards that are sent to each sales rep over a period of five months.

The audio program allows the traveling sales rep to listen to the features and benefits of a specific product anytime he or she wishes....but the real intent is to listen right before making the sales call, thus getting the information on-demand just before it will be needed. Hopefully, the rep has given time to sales preparation prior to getting in the car, but the reality is that many sales presentations are made with a minimum of preparation. The SalesMaker "Tune-ups" are designed to be 20 minutes or less — to address the attention span issues and also so they're short enough to be listened to while driving across town, or just before making the presentation.

Salesmaker audio programs are designed to cover all the features/benefits that make the product unique...that way the reps knows which are the really important benefits to cover and which features are the "me too" ones.

The laminated TIPS card is a further condensation of the main points to be covered in a sales presentation. They're easy to review while waiting (usually in front of the receptionist) to see the prospect and they're also easy to use while making the presentation.

The "reminder" postcards help fight the "forgetting curve." Ideally, a rep will listen to the Salesmaker audio program as many times as it takes to integrate all the important features/benefits into his or her presentation, but the reality is that the rep will eventually be distracted by the other plethora of products he or she must sell. We send them a postcard in two weeks, six weeks, and twenty weeks from receipt of the tape to remind them of the benefits of re-listening to the audio program. That gives them increased retention, reinforcement, more sales, and additionally, the manufacturer gets more "mindshare" and ultimately attention for the product and increased sales.

Who needs this intervention? This raises an interesting point in the sense of "whose problem is this?" It could be said that the rep has the need because he or she needs to give better presentations, and the rep can keep his or her job better if he or she sells more, but individual reps cannot logically fund the cost of a training system production. The same would be true for distributors of products; they know they could benefit from training aids, but they won't pay for them. So who has the need and who will pay the bill is an interesting issue, but reality intervenes and gives us an answer we can sink our teeth into.

The manufacturer depends on salespeople, no matter how many different types or levels there happen to be, to make effective presentations. A manufacturer can spread the cost of creating a Salesmaker Acceleration System, for a specific product, over the large number of a national sales force. Manufacturers have the need and can easily justify the nominal expense per salesperson and manufacturers also benefit from the additional attention (mindshare) that is generated for their product.

Some Examples:

A manufacturer of medical equipment launches a new product. They have their national sales force. Their product line is already broad and diverse. The reps travel heavily and are home little and in the office even less. When are they going to read the three-ring binder or sit down and watch the video? An audio program is convenient and is listened to while driving; absolutely no productive time is taken away from selling, office work, or family time!

A manufacturer of heating and air conditioning equipment launches a new incentive program. They have their own company managers, employ a national sales force of Independent Manufacturers 'Agents (who call on distributors), and the distributors themselves. The incentive program is fairly complex and needs to be sold through every level of distribution, including installing dealers. Literature is provided, but who's reading it? An audio program hits them where they all live...in their cars!

A manufacturer of electrical relays launches a new product. They have a small management team and depend entirely on their national sales force of "Independent Manufacturers Agents." These agents represent several, if not many, noncompeting lines. The manufacturer has the dual challenge of providing product knowledge and competing for mindshare. A Salesmaker Audio Program delivers the information that allows the reps to be knowledgeable and successful...and concentrate on the lines that they know the most about and are comfortable with....and spend more time selling.

A manufacturer of pumps finds that their distributors (who carry directly competing lines of pumps) would sell more of their pumps if the reps knew the product line better. SalesMaker Acceleration System facilitates better product knowledge which increases comfort level which means more time spent promoting the product, better presentations, and increased sales. The ballpark costs for Salesmaker Acceleration Systems are about $3,500 which usually covers a full program for 100 salespeople, including scripting, recording by voice talents, music where appropriate, cassette labels, packaging, TIPS cards, and the three reminder postcards.

The development time is usually about four weeks. This usually includes two weeks to develop a program from provided print collateral, videos, and phone interviews and two weeks to produce and duplicate audio programs from the date of script approval.

What does the client have to provide? The client must provide sufficient development materials, a sales force of sufficient numbers to make development feasible, and approve voice talent, script, label copy, and color coordination of packaging.

The process can be done via fax, email, or FED EX™. The vendors have created over 100 programs and provided programs to over 45,000. Client companies include electrical, building products, medical, insurance, banking, chemical, process control, air conditioning, greeting cards, recreational, powertools, handtools, and flow control.

This is another great example of enabling learning outside of a classroom and providing access to the users when and where they need it. Even if that means it's in a car going 65 miles per hour north on Interstate 95.

Audio Books

I've mentioned several times that time is a precious commodity and will get more precious as the complexity of our lives increases in parallel with the demands we must address. Part of the complexity that many people deal with in today's work environment involves commuting. People commute in a variety of ways to get to work including cars, buses, trains, ferries, bikes, motorcycles, etc. In many more urban locations, traffic can be severe enough that commuters spend more than an hour commuting each way. People also often have to commute to field-based locations to manage corporate accounts, or coach people, or to land new accounts. But lots of time spent getting to work can be used effectively…getting *to learn*.

Recently, there has been a boom in the audio book industry. Here in Austin, Texas, for example, there is an Audio Bookstore rental store. Customers rent audio books (like videos at Blockbuster™) that are in cassette or CD format so that they can listen to them over a couple of week's time and then return them. The nice thing about this is that there are literally thousands of titles and topics to choose and you could *listen* to several good books a week or month, just in your commute time. There are the latest fiction bestsellers, but there are also the latest hot business books and self-help books on personal finance, psychology, and negotiations, just to name a few. The customer can check these out and listen while they go to and from work, and it's safe. People driving cars don't have to worry about trying to drive a car and read a book — it's not really a good thing to do.

If you don't have an Audio Bookstore in your town, most public libraries carry audio books now. All major bookstores like Barnes and Nobles, Borders, etc., carry them. And of course, you can order them directly online from Amazon.com, Books a Million, and other online bookstores. This may seem like something that doesn't appeal to you, however, I ask that you just try it once and I think you'll be hooked.

High-Tech Examples
Training Consultant Assimilation Using Microsoft Outlook™

I am always looking for ways to integrate tools that are used in the workplace to help people learn. I was able to create a solution like this using Microsoft Outlook™. This application is a powerful task, contact, time, and electronic mail management system. Since people across the company are using it, I thought it would be great to use to help manage the learning process for participants. So, I decided to try it for a training consultant assimilation program. Here's how it works.

I created a Coach's Guide for coaches to use to help guide the assimilation process using Microsoft Outlook™. It gives a background and ground rules for the assimilation program. It delineates how to assign tasks and to track progress of the individual(s) that is/are being assimilated. It provides a baseline list of recommended tasks for the new training consultant to complete. Files, attachments, URLs, and other information can be attached in the task that gets assigned to the participant. The coach uses the Coach's Guide and the Learning Guide to describe the assimilation process to the new training consultant. The Learning Guide can be customized for the learner based on his or her experience since it is in a Microsoft Word™ document template.

The Learning Guide is similar to the Coach's Guide except that it shows the learner how assimilation tasks will come to the desktop. There are reference materials listed, recommended tasks to complete, and a complete description of how the learner will complete the assimilation process. The learner can track his or her progress by checking the task list. The system makes discussions on the assimilation occur much quicker, since both the learner and coach can see continuous up-to-date progress.

The next two sections offer the Coach's Guide and the Learning Guide for the Training Consultant Assimilation program I am using.

> **Learning Byte**   *The most innovative learning solution you can build or buy is useless without the complementary learning need. Don't force fit solutions to nonexistent problems. If a television set fell into the hands of some people 300 years ago, it wouldn't have been an innovation, it would have been something to display plates on.*

TRAINING CONSULTANT COACHING GUIDE – HOW TO EFFICIENTLY ASSIMILATE YOUR NEW TRAINING CONSULTANT

How to Use This Coaching Guide

Background

Helping to get a new Training Consultant at Dell Computer Corporation assimilated is one of the most exciting, challenging, and demanding roles you can play in the company. Depending on the employee's background, you may spend a fair amount of time working with him or her to get to the point where he or she is self-sufficient. This Coaching Guide is meant to help you… help them. It is a tool that will help you assign tasks, monitor progress, and mentor your new Training Consultant.

Ground Rules

You are a key player in the assimilation of your new Training Consultant. You will need to work closely with your Training Consultant to distribute learning opportunities, conduct one on ones, and help create the consultant's network.

Meet regularly with the training consultant to discuss progress and to answer questions that he or she may have.

MS Outlook is a key part of the implementation of this assimilation process. If you aren't familiar with how the tasks section of MS Outlook works, you may want to review it with someone. The basic steps needed to implement this program will be included here.

The Coaching Guide provides some generic tasks that will apply to most Training Consultants at Dell. However, this guide can be customized to input more segment-specific or function-specific tasks.

Learning Opportunities

One way you will get to distribute learning opportunities is through the use of task assignments right to your Consultant's desktop. You will send your Training Consultant electronic reminders of specific learning opportunities. This is what the reminder looks like:

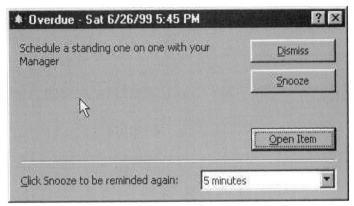

If the Consultant can't complete the task right away, he or she can select snooze so the reminder will minimize and reappear at a pre-arranged time later.

It is important that the Consultant open the task item, because there could be explicit additional information to help him or her complete the task.

When the Training Consultant completes a task, mark the status as complete. This will send a note back to you to track progress.

Notice the Category "Training Consultant Assimilation." This will help you quickly see all tasks associated with this assimilation. You'll be able to print a list of all tasks completed for verification and tracking.

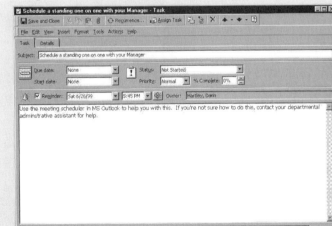

Files, web site addresses, and other information could be included.

Assigning Tasks

You've seen what an incoming reminder looks like for the Training Consultant, but how do you do that? It's pretty easy.

1. Go to tasks in MS Outlook.
2. Click on **File**, then **New Task**. (Or you can click on the icon with the clipboard and checkmark in the upper left-hand corner.) This is what you will see:

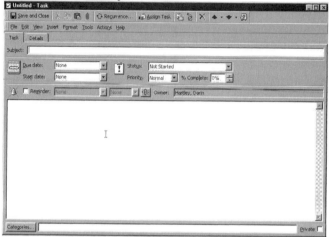

3. Enter the subject (or task statement).
4. Select a due date.
5. Assign the task by clicking on **Assign Task** on the menu bar.

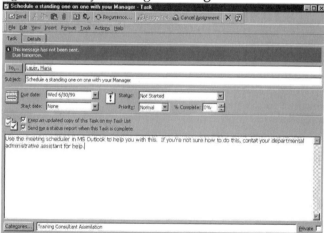

6. Enter the name of the person to send it to. Ensure you have a Training Consultant Assimilation Category, and assign a due date. Check both boxes about updated copies and status reports. Then send!

**Tracking
Completion of
Assignments**

You may want to track tasks you've assigned related to this assimilation. In order to do that, you can go into your Outlook Task list and view tasks by category. Here's how:

1. Go to tasks.
2. Click on **View** in the menu bar.
3. Hold left mouse button down and go to **Current View**.
4. Click on **By Person Responsible**. Here you will see people whom you have assigned tasks to and current status. This is a great way to track individual progress on assigned tasks.

Print this page when you have one-on-one meetings with your training consultants to discuss progress and issues.

**Using the Soft
Copy of This
Guide**

If you view the soft copy of this Learning Guide, you will notice that some of the resources are underlined and blue. These are hyperlinks that will take you directly to the web site in question, if you're online.

Getting Started

You've got the basic information you need to get started on coaching your new Training Consultant. The following pages will highlight the types of tasks and learning opportunities that your Consultants will probably get a chance to complete. The timeline that you have the Consultants complete these in can vary depending on your business segment, level, and the needs of your department. There are no two assimilation processes that are exactly alike.

So, good luck and let's start the assimilation.

Learning Content and Opportunities

	Tasks	Point of Contact or Resources
Administrative items you'll need completed if you're a new hire *Use this guide and the steps shown in the previous section to assign these and other tasks to your Training Consultant. The last section of the guide has a place where you can add any other tasks, too.*	1. Locate your departmental administrative assistant. 2. Get any office supplies you may need. 3. Order your business cards. 4. Draw your organizational chart (include the two organizations above your current organization). 5. Get a long distance calling code. 6. If you're not familiar with MS Outlook, sit down with your Admin and get a brief tutorial (or schedule a class). 7. Ensure you have a travel profile completed. 8. Use Computer Support number if needed.	1. Manager 2. Admin 3. Admin 4. Manager/Admin 5. Admin 6. Admin/Dell Learning Course Catalog 7. Admin/Maritz Travel 8. 8-4040
Work Site Orientation	1. Locate conference rooms and training rooms in building you are located in. Determine which conference rooms you can use routinely for your department. 2. Discuss locations of Dell campuses including Brockton, Braker (including manufacturing), Parmer, Metric 12, Corridor Park, DFO, Old Town Square, RR1, RR2, RR2E, RR2W, RR3, RR5, RR7, RR8, and Quarry Lake. When meetings call for it, visit the various Dell locations. 3. Locate your Building Services Coordinator (BSC) and have a brief discussion on security including temporary badges and escort requirements.	1. Admin 2. Admin/Manager/Dell Building Maps 3. BSC

Specific Site Tours of Interest	1.	Tour Metric 12 Facility.	1.	Metric 12 rep
	2.	Tour the Executive Briefing Center.	2.	Executive Briefing Center Rep
	3.	Tour Quarry Lake business offices and training rooms.	3.	Dell Learning Ed Services

Understanding Dell Culture	1. Take the Dell Business Model, online.	1. Dell Business Model Site or read *Direct from Dell*, by Michael Dell
	2. Review the Code of Conduct.	2. Code of Conduct online
	3. Cruise the Corporate Communications site.	3. Corporate Communications
	4. If you haven't been to one yet, ask one of your co-workers about our annual rallies at the Erwin Center.	4. Manager or co-workers
	5. Review Michael Dell's Top Ten List of Things to Do for 1999.	5. Manager
	6. Take the Know the Net course online.	6. Manager
Departmental Orientation	1. Identify and meet with your co-workers in your department.	1. Manager/Admin
	2. Get on your departmental staff meeting schedule.	2. Admin
	3. State the mission and vision of the department.	3. Manager
	4. Identify the other departments that you work closest with. Identify key contacts in each of those departments.	4. Manager/Co-Workers
	5. Discuss with manager how your department supports the overall mission and vision of Dell.	5. Manager
	6. Shadow or observe several key positions that you support in your department.	6. Manager/ Employee's Manager
	7. Identify standing operational meetings and other cyclical meetings the department holds.	7. Manager

Business Segment Orientation	1. Identify the mission and vision of the business segment. 2. Identify the segment Senior VP and his or her staff. 3. Identify the major functions within your business segment, such as IT, Marketing, Sales, Finance, etc. 4. Review product information. 5. Examine your business segment's Intranet and Internet sites. See sales site to the right as an example.	1. Manager 2. Manager 3. Manager 4. http://inside.us.dell.com/dellu/peak/index.asp and http://www.dell.com/products/ 5. http://inside.us.dell.com/sales/
Dell Learning Orientation	1. Identify the mission and vision of Dell Learning. 2. Identify the organizational chart for Dell Learning. 3. Describe the functions of the Program Managers and who they are. 4. Describe the functions of each of the four teams in Dell Learning Corporate including: Dell Learning Technology Services, Dell Learning Solutions, Education Services, and New Product Training. 5. Describe the training registration system at Dell. 6. Describe the Pay As You Use (PAYU) philosophy of Dell Learning. 7. Obtain schedules for Extend Staff meetings, Operations Reviews, and Senior Staff meetings if appropriate.	1. Dell Learning web site 2. Jack Tootson 3. Jack Tootson 4. Manager Ed Services, Darin Hartley, David Jedrziewski, or John Reynolds 5. http://inside.us.dell.com/dellu/dpt/ 6. Manager 7. Manager
Other or Misc.		

USEFUL REFERENCE MATERIALS

Books

Meister, Jeanne C. (1998) *Corporate Universities*. McGraw-Hill.

Robinson, Dana Gaines, and Robinson, James C. (1998) *Moving from Training to Performance*. Berrett-Koehler Pub.

Schank, Roger. (1997) *Virtual Learning*. McGraw-Hill.

The Manager's Pocket Guide Series. HRD Press.

Web Sites

www.astd.org

www.trainingnet.com

www.hrdpress.com

Magazines

Inside Technology Training Magazine
TRAINING
Corporate University Review

Assessments

Management Development Questionnaire (MDQ). (1998) HRD Press.

Performance Skills Leaders. (1997) HRD Press.

Learning Styles Questionnaire (LSQ). (1999) HRD Press.

Dealing with Conflict Instrument (DWCI). (1999) HRD Press.

TRAINING CONSULTANT LEARNING GUIDE – WHAT YOU NEED TO KNOW... NOW

How to Use This Learning Guide

Background

Being a Training Consultant at Dell Computer Corporation is one of the most exciting, challenging, and demanding roles you can play in the company. You have to have a host of skills and competencies in order to analyze business problems, design solutions, manage development or acquisition of the solution, implement the solution, and measure the success of the solution relative to key business metrics.

If you've moved into a Training Consultant role from a Subject Matter Expert (SME) role previously, you may have questions about how to take your rich business-based expertise and quickly leverage it with performance improvement strategies to quickly catalyze business improvements.

Ground Rules

Much of the learning in this assimilation program will be self-directed. You will need to review this Learning Guide, seek out one-on-one meetings with your immediate manager and other functional specialists and business people in the field. You will need to conduct some research and read books. You will use web sites and maybe attend a conference. You will need to work to build your "consultant" network, since you will not be able to do many things entirely on your own. Finally, ask questions and push back appropriately. If you're not sure about something or have a better way to do something, tell your manager. The key is for you to take charge of your learning and make it fit your specific learning style.

Learning Opportunities

One way you will get to discover learning opportunities is through the use of incoming reminder tasks right to your desktop. Your manager will be using a Coach's Guide to send you electronic reminders of specific learning opportunities for you to take. Like this one below:

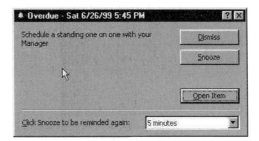

If you can't complete the task right away, you can select snooze so the reminder will minimize and reappear at a pre-arranged time later.

It is important for you to open the task item, because there could be explicit additional information to help you to complete the task.

When you complete a task, mark the status as complete. This will send a note back to your coach so that he or she knows your progress.

Notice the Category "Training Consultant Assimilation." This will help you quickly see all tasks associated with this assimilation. You'll be able to print a list of all tasks completed for verification and tracking.

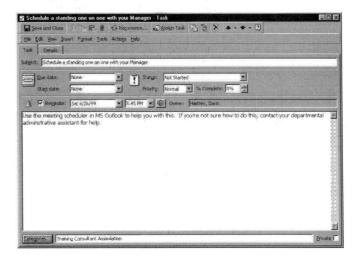

Files, web site addresses, and other information may be included.

Tracking Completion of Assignments	You may want to track your assignments related to this assimilation. In order to do that, you can go into your Outlook Task list and view tasks by category. Here's how:

1. Go to tasks.
2. Click on **View** in the menu bar.
3. Hold left mouse button down and go to **Current View**.
4. Click on **By Category**. Here you will see categories of tasks if you use them, plus one category called Training Consultant Assimilation. In this category are the tasks for your assimilation process.

5. Click on the + sign and see what happens.

You can see that the tasks associated with Training Consultant Assimilation are shown, including status, percent complete, and task detail. You can select any task and open it to see detail.

Additionally, these lists can be printed for you to keep for review or show to your manager.

Using the Soft Copy of This Guide	If you view the soft copy of this Learning Guide, you will notice that some of the resources are underlined and blue. These are hyperlinks that will take you directly to the web site in question, if you're online.
Getting Started	You've got the basic information you need to get started on your assimilation process at Dell. The following pages will highlight the types of tasks and learning opportunities that you will probably get a chance to complete. The timeline that you complete these in can vary depending on your business segment, level, and the needs of your manager. There are no two assimilation processes that are exactly alike.

So, good luck and let's start the assimilation. |

Learning Content and Opportunities

	Tasks	Point of Contact or Resources
Administrative items you'll need completed if you're a new hire	1. Locate your departmental administrative assistant.	1. Manager
	2. Get any office supplies you may need.	2. Admin
	3. Order your business cards.	3. Admin
	4. Draw your organizational chart (include the two organizations above your current organization).	4. Manager/Admin
	5. Get a long distance calling code.	5. Admin
	6. If you're not familiar with MS Outlook, sit down with your Admin and get a brief tutorial (or schedule a class).	6. Admin/Dell Learning Course Catalog
	7. Ensure you have a travel profile completed.	7. Admin/Maritz Travel
	8. Use Computer Support number if needed.	8. 8-4040
Work Site Orientation	1. Locate conference rooms and training rooms in building you are located in. Determine which conference rooms you can use routinely for your department.	1. Admin
	2. Discuss locations of Dell campuses including Brockton, Braker (including manufacturing), Parmer, Metric 12, Corridor Park, DFO, Old Town Square, RR1, RR2, RR2E, RR2W, RR3, RR5, RR7, RR8, and Quarry Lake. When meetings call for it, visit the various Dell locations.	2. Admin/ Manager/ Dell Building Maps
	3. Locate your Building Services Coordinator (BSC) and have a brief discussion on security including temporary badges and escort requirements.	3. BSC
Specific Site Tours of Interest	1. Tour Metric 12 Facility.	1. Metric 12 rep
	2. Tour the Executive Briefing Center.	2. Executive Briefing Center Rep
	3. Tour Quarry Lake business offices and training rooms.	3. Dell Learning Ed Services

Understanding Dell Culture	1. Take the Dell Business Model, online.	1. Dell Business Model Site or read *Direct from Dell*, by Michael Dell
	2. Review the Code of Conduct.	2. Code of Conduct online
	3. Cruise the Corporate Communications site.	3. Corporate Communications
	4. If you haven't been to one yet, ask one of your co-workers about our annual rallies at the Erwin Center.	4. Manager or co-workers
	5. Review Michael Dell's Top Ten List of Things to Do for 1999.	5. Manager
	6. Take the Know the Net course online.	6. Manager
Departmental Orientation	1. Identify and meet with your co-workers in your department.	1. Manager/Admin
	2. Get on your departmental staff meeting schedule.	2. Admin
	3. State the mission and vision of the department.	3. Manager
	4. Identify the other departments that you work closest with. Identify key contacts in each of those departments.	4. Manager/Co-Workers
	5. Discuss with manager how your department supports the overall mission and vision of Dell.	5. Manager
	6. Shadow or observe several key positions that you support in your department.	6. Manager/Employee's Manager
	7. Identify standing operational meetings and other cyclical meetings the department holds.	7. Manager
Business Segment Orientation	1. Identify the mission and vision of the business segment.	1. Manager
	2. Identify the segment Senior VP and his or her staff.	2. Manager
	3. Identify the major functions within your business segment, such as IT, Marketing, Sales, Finance, etc.	3. Manager
	4. Review product information.	4. http://inside. us.dell.com/dellu/ peak/index.asp and http://www.dell.com /products/

92

	5. Examine your business segment's Intranet and Internet sites. See sales site to the right as an example.	5. http://inside.us.dell.com/sales/
Dell Learning Orientation	1. Identify the mission and vision of Dell Learning.	1. Dell Learning web site
	2. Identify the organizational chart for Dell Learning.	2. Jack Tootson
	3. Describe the functions of the Program Managers and who they are.	3. Jack Tootson
	4. Describe the functions of each of the four teams in Dell Learning Corporate including: Dell Learning Technology Services, Dell Learning Solutions, Education Services, and New Product Training.	4. Manager Ed Services, Darin Hartley, David Jedrziewski, or John Reynolds
	5. Describe the training registration system at Dell.	5. http://inside.us.dell.com/dellu/dpt/
	6. Describe the Pay As You Use (PAYU) philosophy of Dell Learning.	6. Manager
	7. Obtain schedules for Extend Staff meetings, Operations Reviews, and Senior Staff meetings if appropriate.	7. Manager
Other or Misc.		

Useful reference Materials

Books

Meister, Jeanne C. (1998) *Corporate Universities.* McGraw-Hill.

Robinson, Dana Gaines, and Robinson, James C. (1998) *Moving from Training to Performance.* Berrett-Koehler Pub.

Schank, Roger. (1997) *Virtual Learning.* McGraw-Hill.

The Manager's Pocket Guide Series. HRD Press.

Web Sites

www.astd.org

www.trainingnet.com

www.hrdpress.com

Magazines

Inside Technology Training Magazine

TRAINING
Corporate University Review

Assessments

Management Development Questionnaire (MDQ). (1998) HRD Press.

Performance Skills Leaders. (1997) HRD Press.

Learning Styles Questionnaire (LSQ). (1999) HRD Press.

Dealing with Conflict Instrument (DWCI). (1999) HRD Press.

As you saw from the previous examples, use of corporate tools can be a powerful learning opportunity for your organization because people use these tools on a daily basis.

Online Performance and Learning at BellSouth

BellSouth is a $23 billion international communications company, headquartered in Atlanta, Georgia, providing telecommunications, wireless communications, cable and digital TV, directory advertising and publishing, and Internet and data services to nearly 31 million customers in 19 countries worldwide. The BellSouth Leadership Institute (BSLI) is responsible for providing high-quality management and executive education across the BellSouth companies. Management development courses supplement on-the-job training and technical job training courses, and play an important role in the overall development of management employees

In the fall of 1998, two circumstances arose simultaneously at BellSouth, prompting the need for an online coaching and leadership development system. The two driving issues, and the solution the BellSouth Leadership Institute implemented to address them, are discussed below.

The Challenge

During a routine management needs assessment process, performed by the BellSouth Leadership Institute, a new learning need became evident: the need for a just-in-time coaching resource to supplement classroom training experiences and supervisory support.

To ensure it's meeting the needs of its management employees, BSLI carefully gathers needs assessment data approximately every 18 months. During the latest assessment, which started in the spring of 1998 and was completed later that fall, BSLI sent surveys to a statistically valid random sample of first- and second-level supervisors, and followed these surveys up with focus groups to discuss findings in more detail.

One of the key findings was that supervisory managers need just-in-time learning resources to address critical problems and issues. The managers reported that they still value the face-to-face training programs offered by BSLI, but they are unable to participate in group classroom sessions for *all* of their learning needs, and the classroom sessions are not always timely enough to meet immediate needs.

This need was exacerbated by the fact that BellSouth is hiring first-level managers at a fast rate to prepare for a significant volume of expected retirements in the first few years of the next century. BSLI believes that just-in-time learning resources for these new managers will be critical, because their learning curve is steep.

The second factor driving BellSouth to the implementation of an online learning system occurred at about the same time. BellSouth's senior leadership team re-assessed organizational goals to bring them in line with the company's vision for the future. As a result, they devised with three organizational aspirations:

1.   A Great Place to Work: Top 100 Employer
2.   Tops in Customer Loyalty
3.   Financial Excellence

BellSouth recognizes that a significant factor in employee satisfaction is the opportunity to learn and develop. The 1998 BellSouth Employee Satisfaction survey revealed that 68 percent of employees would like more opportunities for training.

"We want to meet our managers' needs for training opportunities," said Scott Boston, Director – Management Training and Development, BSLI. "We believe that if our employees are satisfied, then they'll work harder to satisfy our customers. Our new online coaching system helps support our company's first and second aspirations."

The Solution

At first, Boston and team believed they would offer a medley of online courses to meet the just-in-time learning needs of leaders. They planned to offer a wide selection of online courseware, some developed internally and some externally, from which managers could select learning tools. They then realized that a more appropriate response to the stated needs of supervisory managers was an Electronic Performance Support System (EPSS) that provides easily searched and retrieved, small bytes of learning. The managers didn't need to complete a structured online course for every learning need. Rather, they needed fast coaching resources and job-transfer tools for quick skill application. As previously discussed, people are smart enough to use smaller bits of knowledge to perform a new skill without knowing all of the theory and background behind a topical area.

BSLI found a solution in OPAL^{SM}, *Online Performance and Learning*, from Development Dimensions International (DDI), headquartered in Pittsburgh, Pennsylvania. OPAL is a rare example of an EPSS for human performance skills, also called soft skills, and it dovetails nicely with the classroom training offered by BSLI (some of which also comes from DDI). It is made up of three components: *Advisor*, which offers just-in-time coaching arranged by work situation; *Developer*, which provides competency-based skill development resources; and *Assessor*, which provides learners with a fast and easy, individually driven method for collecting feedback on competencies to drive development activities. Developer and Assessor are described more fully at the end of this chapter.

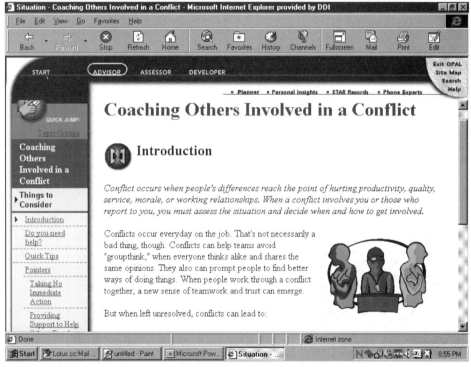

OPAL Advisor provides coaching for hundreds of challenging work situations. Here is the introduction page for a section on helping others resolve conflict.

To meet employees' immediate needs, BSLI chose to implement OPAL Advisor for the entire management population in all thirty-six BellSouth companies. Several companies also opted to promote OPAL to their non-management employees.

OPAL Advisor provides a range of learning resources that employees can access on a just-in-time basis. Employees get practical tips, guidelines, pointers, and pitfalls with a click of the mouse. In addition, there are more than 200 skill-building tools, such as checklists, road maps, guidelines for action, planners, tip sheets, and intervention techniques, that are designed to be used on the job to help people use what they learn. Also included are self-assessments, which help employees determine where to focus their learning. The topics in Advisor cover a wide variety of job situations, from rescuing difficult meetings to being a good team member to developing ideas in a discussion.

The topics are grouped under thirteen skill areas:

- Change
- Coaching
- Collaborating
- Conflict
- Core Interpersonal Skills
- Customer Service
- Delegating
- Interviewing
- Meetings
- Performance Management
- Productivity
- Stress Management
- Teams

BSLI found that these topics support the learning needs most requested by BellSouth supervisory managers, and that the content is relevant and comprehensive. "BSLI is impressed with the variety of suggestions and performance tools offered with each situation, and has found OPAL to be as beneficial to managers who have only a few minutes, as to those who need more comprehensive coaching and guidance," said Boston.

The Implementation

BSLI analyzed OPAL's content to ensure it supported BellSouth's policies and language/terminology. They also put OPAL through usability tests and a pilot to make sure that it would be valuable and user-friendly to their target population. OPAL was seen by the test and pilot participants to be an effective and usable tool. The results helped drive communication strategy and positioning, as well as customization of the system for greater ease-of-use and clarity. BSLI performed some simple customization, while DDI helped with more advanced applications.

BSLI conducted usability studies on six management employees from different BellSouth entities. Employees were given sample tough work scenarios and asked to solve problems through advice found in OPAL. The participants found the site easy to navigate and the content helpful.

After receiving the favorable usability study results, BSLI conducted a pilot on 3,000 management and nonmanagement employees at BellSouth Advertising and Publishing Company (BAPCO), in early spring 1999. During this pilot, communication and orientation materials, as well as OPAL itself, were evaluated. Feedback from the management employees was positive.

BSLI decided to target management employees with the new online training package. The staff sent a communications package, complete with a cover letter, brochure, and a laminated helpful hints card, to all BellSouth first- and second-level managers in June 1999.

BSLI has recently identified an additional application for OPAL at BellSouth, which is currently under consideration. Future management employees at BellSouth go through an assessment before being considered for a management role. BellSouth believes OPAL can help prepare the test participants for the evaluation, and enhance pass ratios.

The Early Results and Future Measurement

Although long-term impact has yet to be measured, BellSouth has received positive survey and anecdotal feedback from BAPCO employees. Management users found that OPAL is particularly helpful when they face a discussion with an employee or co-worker of a challenging nature, such as poor performance, work habits, or personal problems that interfere with productivity.

BAPCO employees also found that OPAL's performance support tools are very valuable. One tool in particular, a Meeting Planner found in the Leading Successful Meetings portion of Advisor, was reported by numerous managers to cut meeting time in half, which can obviously lead to significant pay-off in productivity gains across large numbers of people. Users additionally reported that OPAL is easy to learn and navigate without formal training.

These early results are positive indicators for a successful ongoing OPAL implementation. BSLI plans to continue to gather feedback from several sources and create monthly reports on the progress of the OPAL program. Users will have three ways to offer feedback on OPAL to BSLI: a "feedback icon," a hotline, and the next needs assessment survey, during which feedback for OPAL will be queried specifically. The BSLI measurement team will analyze results from all these sources, and evaluate usage via a web tracking system to drive the monthly reports.

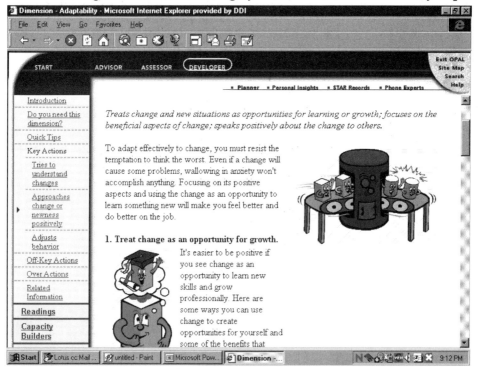

This screen shows a portion of OPAL Developer's Adaptability competency area. In the main page, learners find advice for approaching change or newness positively. In the content outline on the left, there are links to many other learning tools, including suggested readings and skill-building exercises.

The ultimate goal is for supervisory managers to report improvements in managerial effectiveness and greater availability of appropriate, just-in-time learning opportunities. "We look forward to analyzing the monthly reports," Boston said. "Based on the results, we may further customize OPAL to meet our employees' needs."

More about OPAL

In addition to OPAL Advisor, OPAL offers two other components, each of which offers different types of online development support.

Providing time-efficient, just-what's-needed learning, OPAL *Developer* helps employees understand and gain skill in a variety of business competencies. Employees select the competency they want to develop; they can then read a complete, concise definition of the competency, and click to Quick Tips for on-the-spot help. They can thoroughly investigate each of the competency's key behaviors to learn exactly what's expected on the job, including off-key actions and over-actions, behaviors that either fall short of the mark or go too far. To further reinforce their knowledge and transfer it to the job, they can work through a range of over 300 capacity-building exercises.

Developer fosters both intellectual understanding as well as the skills to put that knowledge into practice. To develop their skills, learners can explore OPAL Developer's thirty-two competencies, which are customizable to reflect an organization's existing competency models:

- Adaptability
- Aligning Performance for Success
- Building a Successful Team
- Building Customer Loyalty
- Building Partnerships
- Building Strategic Working Relationships
- Building Trust
- Coaching
- Sales Ability/ Persuasiveness
- Collaboration
- Contributing to Team Success
- Continuous Improvement
- Continuous Learning
- Customer Focus
- Decision making
- Delegating Responsibility
- Developing Others
- Follow-up
- Formal Presentation

- Gaining Commitment
- Impact
- Information Monitoring
- Initiating Action
- Innovation
- Leading through Vision and Values
- Managing Conflict
- Managing Work
- Oral Communication
- Negotiation
- Planning and Organizing
- Tenacity
- Written Communication

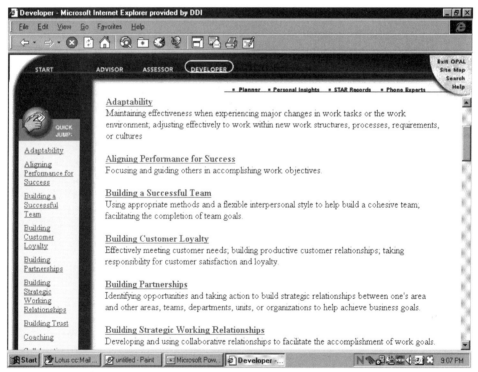

OPAL Developer provides learning and development tools for a variety of work competencies or skills.

OPAL *Assessor* is an online tool employees can use to create flexible assessment surveys designed to target strengths and development areas within a broad range of competencies and associated key actions, the specific behaviors that make up the competency. Users create their own self- or self-plus-other surveys by clicking through OPAL's easy-to-follow prompts. They choose what competencies and key actions they'll be evaluated on, and indicate who will receive the survey. OPAL does the rest. It sends the survey out, logs who has or has not responded, and creates easy-to-read reports of the results. Survey respondents are anonymous; the employee initiating the survey doesn't see individual ratings, only compiled results from all respondents.

The employee can view detailed ratings of all the competencies and key actions, a prioritized list of strengths and weaknesses, and a self-versus-others comparison of all the competencies and key actions. The survey reports also have hyperlinks that take the learner instantly to OPAL Developer for immediate online help with strengthening specific competencies.

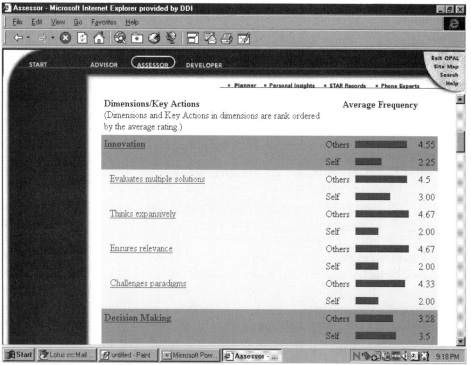

OPAL's Assessor provides an easy-to-read graphical report of feedback data, from which learners can hotlink into Developer to act on the feedback.

BellSouth is considering OPAL Developer and Assessor for future implementation.

Company Information
Based in Pittsburgh, Pennsylvania, Development Dimensions International (DDI) provides integrated human resource solutions to organizations in over seventy countries around the world. DDI's human resource experts help companies put the right people with the right skills and motivations into the right jobs at the right time. Since opening in 1970, DDI has assisted more than 16,000 organizations around the world improve their business performance.

Digital Lava's Video Visor

On-Demand Research Data
CBS, NBC, The WB, MTV. These are just a few of the clients that depend on ASI Entertainment's research. As one of the oldest and largest entertainment research firms in America, ASI provides its clients with important research detailing audience responses to a variety of television programming. In a high-pressure, ratings-driven industry like television, ASI needed a way to quickly and effectively provide its clients with research that would allow them to make critical programming decisions. In the past, reams of paper and accompanying videotapes detailing audience feedback would arrive on ASI clients' desks. Buried in that research was the specific information the clients sought.

Digital Lava offered a unique solution: the incorporation of all research information into an interactive desktop video presentation. By using Digital Lava's Video Publishing suite of tools, ASI now provides its clients with a way to interactively view, analyze, search, annotate, and visually interpret the meaning of audience research data. One of the most significant benefits of Digital Lava's software is the opportunity it gives ASI clients to quickly identify sections of research without having to wade through bulky documents and analysis. For example, a scene including a controversial character or the music played during a particular scene can be immediately pinpointed and viewed.

ASI has several theaters where audiences (representing various demographic segments) view television programs and movies and simultaneously move dials based on their responses (positive or negative) to the content they are viewing. Based on these responses, graphs are created which are then married with the corresponding video using Digital Lava's vPrism software. The combined video and meta data (text, notes, and links) create a "VideoCapsule." Digital Lava's VideoVisor software is the desktop tool that allows ASI clients to view these VideoCapsules. Delivered via CD-ROM on the same day as the session, the VideoCapsules provide valuable "just in time" data to ASI's media clients worldwide.

The technology also has applications in the training and learning field.

How Dell Learning Has Used Video-Visor to Enable On-Demand and Distance Learning

John Coné was asked by some of our counterparts in Dell New Zealand to make a presentation on distance learning to a polytechnic group in Queensland, New Zealand. A trip to New Zealand would use up an entire week's worth of time. There would be two days of travel to and from New Zealand plus the day to spend at the conference. John couldn't dedicate this kind of time for the effort because of conflicts, so I offered Digital Lava's Video Visor as a solution to the problem.

I touched based with the folks in New Zealand and told them about our dilemma and made the recommendation to use the Video Visor product. They were interested and after answering some questions opted to use the Video Visor presentation for the conference. My team worked with John Coné to develop a presentation, arranged the videotaping session (it was done in one take), and worked with the Digital Lava project team to create the final product. The Digital Lava team digitized the video, created the audio tracks and transitions, and transcribed the text of the discussion all in less than a week. The people in New Zealand were able to use the Video Visor presentation for the conference as planned with no hitches.

About Digital Lava

Digital Lava Inc., a Los Angeles, California–based company, was founded in 1995 to create innovative integrated video solutions that leverage the latest in compression, management, database, and delivery technologies. They have video-publishing tools with intuitive interfaces that integrate digital video with relational databases. They have created software that re-purposes, publishes, and deploys digital video data and related information across workgroups and corporate enterprises. Digital Lava Solutions publish and distribute a wide variety of interactive video programs complete with multiple language support and full World Wide Web integration.

How Video Visor Works

Digital Lava's Video Visor™ is a powerful client-side application that puts the power of digitized video in the hands of the end user (see the screen shot below.

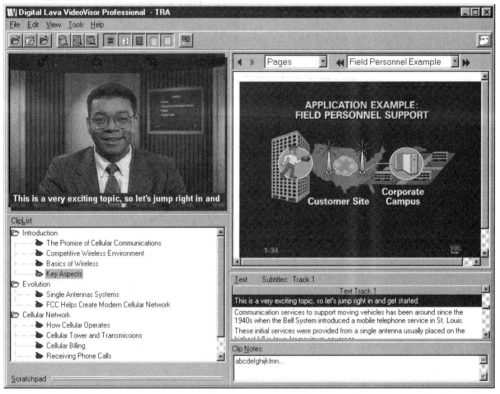

As you can see from the picture above, the application is divided into several major sections. In the upper left quadrant of the application is the default video area. This is where a high-quality thirty frame per second digitized video can be viewed. There are controls under the video window (not shown here) that are used to drive the video, like those on a VCR. This screenshot also shows how subtitles can be used in the video. This is a nice touch if you want to have subtitles in another language from that of the video. One other great feature of this product is that the video can be expanded to full size with no loss in video quality.

In the lower left quadrant are topical areas included on the disk. The end user can quickly maneuver from one topic to another by clicking on the topic. From the screenshot above, you can see that "Key Aspects" is highlighted. This section of clip is running. The user could quickly jump to "Cellular Billing" or any of the other topical areas with a mouse click.

In the upper right quadrant is the application or slide area. Here the end user can view associated slides, applications, web pages, etc., that are associated with this content. It is a live application window, so if a web site is in this area, the dynamic functionality of the web can be harnessed. For example, you might have some content that is relatively static, but some additional content that changes rapidly, for instance, new product information. This tool allows you to digitize the more static content and to link to more dynamic web pages. It can also launch applications such as MS Word™, MS Excel™, etc. Finally, in this section, a person can advance to various parts of the presentation by selecting the "Pages" or "Topics" region at the top.

In the lower right quadrant is the text transcription. Every thing that is said in the digitized presentation is captured there. The text being spoken is highlighted as in the screen shot. The end user can also jump around to various sections by clicking on different topics. There is also a section below that can be used to capture notes about the particular topic in question. These can be referenced later.

Some other functionality includes a customizable interface. The user can shrink and enlarge the various viewing panes inside the Video Visor application. Also there is a search tool that allows an individual to search for a key word or phrase. Each time the key word or phrase appears it will show up in the queue. The user can select found words and jump right to that portion of the clip.

DigiCard - The Credit Card-Sized CD ROM from CAE Media

Several years ago at a conference I met Allen Fahden, one of the keynote speakers and author of *Innovation On-Demand*. After his presentation I met him in a social setting and introduced myself. I pulled out my traditional business card and gave it to him. He said, "Wait,

I'll get you one of mine." As he said this, he pulled one of the largest wads of two-dollar bills I had ever seen from his breast pocket and gave one to me. I remember it like it was yesterday. I thought I'd never see a more interesting business card. Well… times are a-changing. I've found the next generation of business card that can double as an on-demand learning tool as well. It's a *DigiCard* from CAE Media.

The DigiCard is a unique cross between a conventional business or credit card (it's actually the same size as a credit card), but combines the multimedia capabilities of a CD-ROM. DigiCards can store up to 30 MB of information including software, multimedia presentations, web sites, audio, video, licensed content, etc. An account executive could hand a potential client a DigiCard that contains multimedia information on the company, a catalog of all products and services, personal access to insider information, an email link, and access to corporate web sites. In the training arena, an entire forty-hour course's worth of materials, reading, job aids, and pre- and post-testing information could be included on one disk. The possibilities are nearly limitless. The DigiCard works with any CD-ROM player or audio CD player that has a spindle or a CD tray.

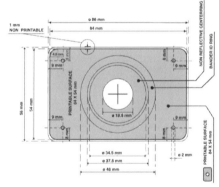

Nexus Technology, Inc., came to CAE Media to improve their corporate identity and have a CD produced that they could use in their exhibit booth at an upcoming tradeshow. Nexus, a SAP-R/3 partner (SAP is an extremely powerful enterprise database application), formed in 1996 to provide consulting on SAP services and products. The organization has evolved into Enterprise Applications Consulting in supporting technical requirements for SAP-R/3 implementations. Nexus needed something high-tech and lively to match the services they provide and the pace of their clients' businesses. During early stages of the project, the idea of using the DigiCard was presented and quickly gained momentum. The possibility of distributing a multimedia presentation featuring the company's services on a high-tech business card appealed to the Nexus management.

While work continued on the CD, CAE Media began working on a presentation and look for Nexus' new corporate logo and their DigiCard. Nexus honed in on the strength of the DigiCard, a personalized portable media (and learning) tool, guaranteed to be noticed. If people won't look at what you want them to see, it doesn't matter how powerful or compelling the intended message is. Putting a message on something so unique was sure to get the audience interested. If the material is also entertaining and succinctly informative, the CD distributor has a winning combination. Empowering the viewer to respond directly via email or allowing the viewer to access a web site via a hyperlink adds a premium to the cards' viability.

The business card size and shape makes the DigiCard the perfect business-to-business tool and also can be leveraged to enable learning in an organization. Nexus had DigiCards produced for each of their executives and salespeople. The personalized DigiCards immediately set Nexus apart from its competitors. An innovative company sometimes needs an innovative edge to create a wedge opportunity, and one of these innovative edges for Nexus is the DigiCard.

The DigiCard can be used to help promote new products or to kick off new initiatives that are underway. Think of what you did with the last paper-based business cards or job aids that you received. Do you still have them? How valuable are they if you can't find them or you can't discern one business card from the next?

DigiCard pricing has two major components. One component is content creation. The other is duplication costs. When considering content creation, cost is a function of complexity and intensity. A full-blown multimedia presentation including an animated opening with music, video, several screens of information with voice over and hyperlinks to a web site can range from $6,000 to $15,000. Something simpler, like a PowerPoint™ presentation or replication of a web site to the DigiCard, can be done for substantially less money. Replication costs vary with quantity. A minimum order of 500 cards costs between $3.50 and $4.00 per card, and an order of 10,000 cards costs between $1.75 and $1.90 per card.

In summary, the DigiCard from CAE Media can be used in a variety of ways. CAE Media has provided a sample DigiCard with this book for you to investigate. For more information check out the www.caemedia.com web site or call 1-800-627-0033 for more information.

Dell SalesMogatchi

One of my best friends and associates at Dell Computer Corporation, Jefferson Raley (a performance consultant at the time), was asked to help solve a business problem in our Home and Small Business (HSB) segment. The HSB group is the group that you will most likely connect with if you call to order a computer (as an individual) or several or more computers (if you are from a small business). New Hire Sales training for incoming inside sales representatives is a crucial part of ramping these new Dell salespeople up to speed as soon as possible. An important competency for these folks to grasp is task and time management. Darcy Kurtz, HSB's Sales Training Manager, analyzed sales data and realized there was a strong correlation between sales reps who allocate time appropriately on key tasks and sales success on the job. These tasks included responding to inbound phone calls, responding to email, responding to faxes, and responding to held orders (those orders that were waiting on credit approval). She also determined that there was a correlation of proper management of these tasks to the sales rep's commission, the close rate, customer satisfaction, and large opportunity deals.

Jefferson Raley and Darcy met to share findings. They mulled over the financial data. Darcy expressed concern about many new sales reps not being able to manage their time and tasks well. They talked about the issues of training large numbers of inside sales reps as quickly as possible. She didn't have a lot of classroom time to dedicate to this problem (time management is important to our trainers, too!) She was looking for a simple game to help the new sales reps learn optimal time management. Jefferson then had a breakthrough. Digital pets, or giga-pets, or tamagotchies were (and still are) the rage. If you haven't seen these, or haven't bought these for your kids or nieces or nephews, here's how they work. The digital pet has to be fed. It needs water and play time. It needs to get enough rest, etc. There are built-in alarms and reminders to help the gigapet owner remember to complete these tasks. If it gets these things, then the digital pet gets older, and in some cases, the digital pet even evolves. If it doesn't get the things it needs, in appropriate proportions, sadly, it dies. And the owner of the gigapet must start the whole process again.

Jefferson's brilliant learning leap was to build a *Salesmogatchi* for the inside Dell sales representatives. A small desktop interface/application can be loaded on the sales rep's desktop that simulate the tasks that need to be completed (with frequency guidelines), the customer satisfaction, close rates, and gross sales. The goal is to make as much money as possible. To do this you have to maintain customer satisfaction while closing a lot of sales. There are meters on the application and also a cartoon sales rep (you can choose a male or a female rep if you'd like) to show you how you are doing. The sales day is time compressed so that the sales rep can get a sense of the whole selling day in less than thirty minutes.

Calls, emails, and voicemails flood in as soon as the program is started. The sales rep has to balance answering the phone with responding to emails and other tasks. If the phone goes unanswered for too long, customer satisfaction drops. This in turn lowers the close rate (percentage of customers who buy) and reduces amount of money the sales rep makes. But sales reps can't spend all of their time answering the phone either. If they do emails go unanswered and other customers are neglected. Success (as in real life) depends on balancing time among all of the various tasks.

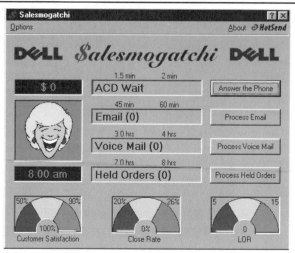

Dell business heuristics were used to calculate gross sales, revenues, close rates, etc., to provide realism for the application. These can be easily adjusted by the training coordinator as Dell's business changes. All of the program logic is run off of a text file that can be edited in any word processor. This keeps the software synchronized with the real world. The better the sales rep manages time and his or her customers, the more sales he or she has, the higher the customer satisfaction, and the higher the close rate, which are all things that are valued very highly at Dell.

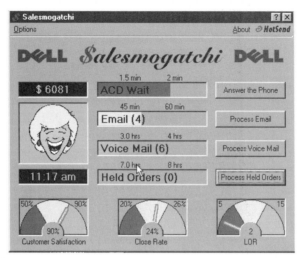

The cost of the project was amazingly small as well. The entire project was developed for under $4,000. Jefferson and Darcy provided design specifications to an outside vendor who provided the custom coding for them on the project. Sales reps and external people that we have shown this application absolutely love it. You can have fun and learn at the same time!

Chatterbots - Virtual Service Reps (Neuromedia.com)

Do you have service centers or call centers in your organization? One thing that happens if you've got one of these are the repetitive questions that the service center will get. For example, in a Human Resources Service Center, a representative might be asked several times a day how to change 401K deductions or how to submit a medical claim or how to get a list of approved doctors in the coverage area. All of these frequently asked questions (FAQs) minimize the amount of valued-added consulting and service these representatives can provide. The FAQs also become taxing for the customer service representatives as the similar questions are asked and answered and asked and answered again and again in a seemingly never-ending loop.

Enter chatterbot technology. Chatterbots use natural language responses to questions using pattern-matching technology to present answers. This is not a search engine. Chatterbots are programmed to note combinations of words, syntax, and word and pattern context to create responses for the end user. There are many chatterbots out there to look at and explore. One is Neuromedia Inc.'s Neuroserver product. This product allows lay folk to create custom chatterbots for their organizations. Go to www.neuromedia.com and try out the virtual service representative there.

Dictionary.com - Online Definitions and Spelling

This example of a high-tech on-demand learning intervention relates to one of the most familiar learning tools of all time, the dictionary. I find myself needing a dictionary on a semi-regular basis at work and at home when I write. I never seem to have one around, or I have the pocket paperback variety, which invariably doesn't have the words I'm trying to spell or define. I've also found that some of the online word processing thesauruses are not as accurate as I'd like either. The solution I've found is a great web site called dictionary.com that helps solve many of my needs.

Dictionary.com is a site with a database-driven dictionary. It can be used to look up words including spelling, definitions, pronunciation, a thesaurus (through theasurus.com), word origins (etymologies... I just looked that up online), and many other tools. If you enter a word and aren't sure of the spelling, the site makes recommendations for words that you can select and check. On the lighter side, there are words of the day, interactive crosswords, and word searches. You can also get words in German, Greek, Latin, and Spanish. It's just a very user-friendly and valuable site.

I have the hyperlink to dictionary.com on my desktop so I can quickly get there from other open applications I am running. It is also wise to add it to your favorites or bookmarks in the browser. Use this tool as you would a regular dictionary when you are working online. You'll return again and again.

IDX Systems Distance Learning Solves a Programming Dilemma

IDX Systems Makes MUMPS Less Painful...From a Distance

IDX Systems Corporation is one of the largest healthcare information systems companies in the country. IDX provides a broad range of functionally rich and highly integrated products designed to meet the evolving needs of integrated delivery networks (that include organizations with in- and outpatient facilities), group practices, management service organizations, hospitals, universities, and health plans.

The IDX mission is to use information technology to maximize value in the delivery of healthcare. IDX develops and implements innovative information solutions that help its customers be more successful improving the quality of care, serving patients more efficiently, reducing costs, and more effectively analyzing their businesses. IDX products are installed at more than 1,650 customer sites nationwide, including more than 250 large group practices that average 345 physicians per group, 270 multi-entity hospital systems, and more than 200 of the top 696 integrated delivery networks. There are approximately 3,500 IDX employees nationwide in ten major office locations.

IDX had several interesting problems to solve back in early 1998. How do you train nearly 900 staff members across the country on a programming language and company programming standards at the same time? Distance Learning (DL), a trend of the late 90's seemed to be the only way to go, but it was a new and foreign concept for the organization.

The Client Support Education Center (CSEC), the primary training and development group for staff at IDX, worked with the Organizational Development (IDX Institute of Technology) staff to design a successful program that will be described below.

Like many of its competitors in the information technology industry, IDX requires some of its staff to learn IDX's programming language to provide its robust client base with decision support for their software. IDX uses MUMPS, or "M," to program its client solutions. Because so few vendors offer M-based solutions, it was necessary for IDX personnel to train its staff on the language conventions and internal programming requirements.

Need for Change

Historically, IDX Systems offered M in a stand-up instruction style. Although the need for M training is present in all offices, course offerings would vary depending on available resources, if any, to conduct the training. Commonly, a stand-up M instructor would be 100 percent dedicated to the instruction of M. This would also cause attrition because of the constant pressure and lack of variability in job roles. Additionally, there was variability from office to office on the specific contents of the M course with variable levels of quality and differing class lengths. M knowledge varies among IDX new hires and staff who use it in their day-to-day roles, thus creating tremendous gaps in the knowledge level of class attendees. The gap was costing IDX money and it needed to be closed to decrease the ramp-up time of new hires. The full-time employee (FTE) requirement for a stand-up program was huge (at least five FTEs) and was inconsistently implemented in the regional office locations. Time taken to bring staff up to speed was often elongated because of the sporadic class offerings and high travel cost for instructors. There were differences in the material obtained by students due to the instructor variability. Finally, when staff first heard about taking a virtual class without an instructor present in the front of the classroom, there was anxiety and hesitation to migrate to this format, probably due to the fear of losing the tangibility of the course. This was going to be a large cultural shift in learning for the students.

Recapping the needs for change:

1.   Available resources were at a premium and travel costs were high.
2.   New hires needed a method to quickly learn M to be productive in their jobs.
3.   IDX was concerned about instructor burnout and meeting FTE requirements.
4.   This was inconsistent communication of information to participants.
5.   Anxiety and fear developed regarding migration to the new format.
6.   Learners' knowledge levels and skill sets varied greatly. Some staff easily completed the course, while others struggled with baseline concepts. The variance would oftentimes slow the class down.

Solution Implementation
The Distance Learning format implementation addressed the six concerns outlined above in the following manner.

1.   Because resources in every office are at a premium, the distance format allows the sharing of resources nationwide. For example, an instructor can live in either Boston or Chicago and facilitate the session in Burlington, Alameda, or Dallas offices concurrently.

2. The DL format allows new hires to take the class within their first three months of employment. Existing employees can take the class at any point during their career to continue to develop their skill sets. IDX currently offers the class every four to six weeks.
3. Instructors can facilitate across time zones and regional offices. This format is conducive to the sharing of resources and prevention of attrition among M instructors. Therefore, instructors have the ability to work on other projects to prevent burnout.
4. Due to the variance in instructors, material may have been missed. The DL format has provided a way to standardize the communication of information to staff. This standardization also benefits potential instructors by giving them a baseline of training information. In addition, IDX developed an instructor's guide to facilitate consistency of information.
5. Anxiety and fear are natural outcomes of change. As time has progressed with the new format, multiple layers in the organization have accepted it. As more staff is exposed to DL classes at IDX, the acceptance level has increased. Expectations are increasing that staff go through this course in an online format. Incremental change is starting to take hold.
6. As with many high-technology organizations, IDX sees a wide variety of skill sets from potential and existing employees. The traditional format of the M class was modularized. In migrating to the DL format, IDX kept the modularization. One of the challenges IDX had to address was the difference between technical and nontechnical staff and their ability to learn and apply the concepts gained in M. The middle modules, although very difficult, are required for the technical staff, while the nontechnical staff was more likely to hit roadblocks. In the stand-up format, the entire class would go through all modules or part of the class would need to wait for the rest to "catch up." The DL format is more flexible by allowing students to move at their own pace. Additionally, staff can be directed to skip modules to complete at a later time.

The final product looks like the illustration on the following page. As shown, it is an Intranet web-based format, which includes links to the general course information, lecture notes, exercises, and routine descriptions. A closer look at the screen below shows the online discussion thread that is viewable by the instructor and participants. IDX has also implemented local mentoring in each office and instructor advising hours to enhance the learning experience while keeping costs down.

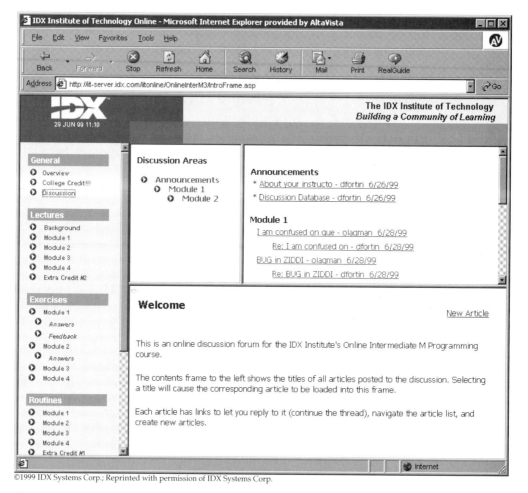

©1999 IDX Systems Corp.; Reprinted with permission of IDX Systems Corp.

Going Forward

As IDX moves forward with the DL M course and other skill offerings at IDX, staff will benefit by receiving training in a standardized fashion with a wider variety of educational choices. These choices will continue to help organizations like IDX develop staff creatively by using alternative learning technologies while keeping within budgetary limits.

Individual Investor Magazine's Investor U — On-Demand Investing Learning

One of the best magazines on the market today for investors is *Individual Investor* magazine. I've been a subscriber and reader of the magazine myself for over two years now and have always appreciated the valuable (literally) information inside its monthly covers. I especially look forward to the coveted Magic 25™ list that comes near the end of the year as a great way to get stock ideas for the coming year. As a reader of the magazine, I noticed they had a web site as well. So, I went to check it out. One of the focal points of the Individual Investor site (www.individualinvestor.com) is the Investor University™ section of the site.

I spoke with Laurie Gordon, the Director of Content Development for Individual Investor's web site, about her inspiration for the information-laden site. She came from an organization that developed online, on-demand learning opportunities for lawyers and was able to leverage her expertise with the magazine's site. Laurie said that initially the Individual Investor online site had an Investing 101 message board in place. On this board, individuals could go read and post questions and answers on an electronic bulletin board about basic investing questions, such as, "How do you read an analyst report?" and "How do you read a balance sheet?" In tandem with this, the Individual Investor site was hosting biweekly investing chat sessions on Yahoo! to provide guidance to investors. All of this information was archived on the web site, but was not truly available in a user-friendly format. That's where Laurie's expertise came in handy. Laurie and her team were able to research the archives, catalog them, and group them into learning bytes that formed mini-lessons on the Individual University™ site. You can see what the page looks like here.

Laurie and her team added another powerful feature — the *Ask our Experts* section of the site. Here, investors can post a question to the site administrator who fields the question to a group of financial analysts to review and answer.

The questions and answers are posted and archived on the site for all investors to see. An example question and part of an answer is below.

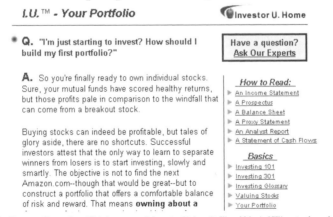

Laurie and the rest of the staff are thrilled with the high-level questions that are being asked and also by the volume of questions. In the first six months since Investor U.™ was launched in January 1999, more than 800 questions have been asked.

Laurie plans to implement synchronous and asynchronous learning on the site in the near future. She is pleased with the Investor U.'s™ success, noting that it is one of the "top five areas of the Individual Investor site that people" go to. She noted that investing clubs use the materials often to help each other get smart about investing, too. So, if you'd like to see a great example of a high-tech on-demand learning solution and want to learn about investing, surf over to www.individualinvestor.com and start learning today.

Summary

I've included a variety of examples of on-demand learning using different industries and applications for you to consider. Some of these may work in your environment. Most likely, you will have to revise the solutions presented here to fit your situation, but at least you'll have some great ideas to consider. Consider this chapter a learning catalyst for your next on-demand learning project. It will probably save you some time.

In the next chapter, I discuss learn2now.com, a site that will help continue the discussion of on-demand learning beyond the publication of the book. If you have a best practice(s) that you would like to share with others out there, read on.

Learning Byte   *Is your learning accessible? Can people get to it when they want to? Or do people have to access it on some predetermined nonflexible schedule? How would you feel if a child of yours was put on a six-week waiting list to be seen for a bout of pneumonia?*

Learn2now.com

There are technological innovations occurring even as this book goes to press. At many colleges, corporations, and government groups innovative thinkers, information technologists, and others are retooling and reinventing tools and performance support systems to make us all smarter and more efficient at what we do and how we learn. In order to help gather and catalog current systems used and to keep this book as relevant and updated as possible, I registered a domain name, learn2now.com, and created a web site to gather this information. Stephanie Powell and her brilliant team at Corporate Images (www.corporateimage.com) helped provide me with the great thematic web site you see at www.learn2now.com. I was pleased with the initial and continuing response from this site. Feel free to go to learn2now.com, browse around, and provide input that can be shared with others out there just-in-time! Also feel free to provide feedback or recommendations on how we can make the site better for everyone.

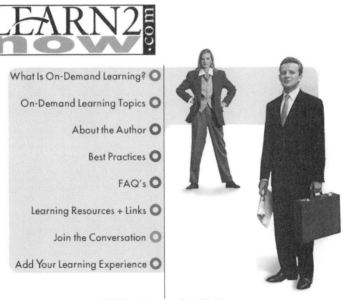

©1999 learn2now.com, Darin Hartley.

Summary

Tomorrow is another day with an endless realm of hope and possibilities surrounding it. The learning landscape we have all been accustomed to and comforted by is going to experience rampant change in the very near future and for a long time to come. As lifelong learning facilitators and professionals, we can all be better prepared for the coming changes in this landscape by sharing these ideas with other learning professionals and training suppliers…starting today. If your current provider or supplier of training services is recommending more and longer classes, it is probably time to start talking with this person(s) as soon as possible to start facilitating change in learning and implementation strategies. If your lifelong learning suppliers refuse to consider alternative learning methods and will not grow with you in your quest to enable on-demand learning, then you need to get other providers who will. One thing I have found to be true in my dealings with suppliers where I currently work is that if you don't ask for certain things, you will never know if people will actually consider doing them. We all make assumptions about what people will say or think before we even ask them the question. So, if you aren't satisfied with the way your learning providers are helping you and your organization learn, ask the providers to change. If they do not change, then you must find learning suppliers who will grow with you and support you.

In retrospect, writing this book (and my previous book) proved to be a great example of learning on-demand. I've always wanted to write a book and have been told by folks that I've got the *knack* for it, so I picked a topic in my field of expertise and where I have a sense of passion and started to conceptualize a plan. I didn't know how to submit a proposal or what format to use, so I searched web sites and called people to get templates and examples to use. I submitted my proposal for my first book to several publishers and received photocopied rejection letters (rejection is even sweeter when it is done in mass) and got a little disgruntled. The idea of writing the book waned under the pressure of eminent project work. Several months passed and I sent the proposal to two publishers after talking to a friend of mine at work. I had two publishing offers within the week and started to write the book. I created a project plan, gathered data and information, and wrote, and wrote, and wrote. I finished the book on time and the book was published as scheduled. When I wrote the first book, I had never been published, I had never been under contract to write a book before, and I had never been through the publishing process. It was all new to me. I had certainly never been to school to get a book published, but I was able to learn what I needed to do, as I needed to do it. I learned on-demand! I did it outside of the work environment, on my own time. No instructor taught me.

With this book, winning the contract was easier to do. However, the complexity of this book is much greater. I've learned about getting rights to publish comic strips, the importance of speaking with the appropriate people in public relations and corporate communications, the importance of barter in projects, and a whole lot about new training technology. I got a domain name registered, built a web site, and worked with various folks to get information and samples for you to read and learn from.

After this book, I've got my mind set on writing a novel. All of my friends are pestering me about writing something they can buy at Barnes and Noble. I jokingly tell them they can get my first book (and soon after publication, my second book) on Amazon.com. They don't care… they want romance or something more mainstream. I'm flattered… and hopeful because I know that I haven't written a published novel before, but I know that I can learn to write one, when I really want to.

I hope that you have found this book insightful and helpful. The ideas presented here are not meant (and were never meant) to be the end all on on-demand learning solutions. I hope they will be catalysts for you and your organization and part of a suite of solutions that you can use as you facilitate learning in your organization. Please feel free to contact me at dhartley@texas.net if you have any questions for me or would like to make contributions to learn2now.com.

> **Learning Byte**   *Can people get just the skill and/or knowledge they need from your learning solution? Or do they have to experience four days of theory before they can safely learn what they need to do?*

Resources

This section of the book contains a variety of resources that will be helpful as you begin to design, develop, and implement on-demand learning solutions.

A Sample Technology-Enabled Learning Strategy

A key in implementing any technology-enabled learning movement in an organization is to have a strategy written. The strategy provides an overall roadmap for the use of technology to enable learning in an organization. If you don't have an overall goal and you start to implement individual solutions, it is very possible that the solutions will be fragmented, dysfunctional, and redundant across the organization. One of the goals of using technology-enabled learning solutions is to minimize those things and have greater impact …quicker.
The following example is one taken from Dell Learning and will give you some ideas for things to include in a strategy. Again, this is just one example.

Dell Learning

Technology-Enabled Learning (TEL) Strategy

Quantifying the Ongoing Requirements and Strategic Direction to Leverage Technology in Learning at Dell

Quantifying the On-Going Requirements and Strategic Direction to Leverage Technology in Learning at Dell

Background

Dell Learning has realized the need for using technology to leverage training impact and delivery velocity for several years now. As early as FY '97, technology-enabled learning solutions started appearing on the scene at Dell.

As the number of new personnel continues to ramp exponentially, coupled with the plethora of new products and service offerings, the necessity of alternative training delivery methods has become overwhelming. Dell Learning has been using more and more technology to enable learning across the enterprise. This has been a good thing for the most part, however, there has never been a clear-cut strategy to develop, implement, and manage technology-enabled learning (TEL) solutions across Dell. In Q1 of FY '00 a team was formed to focus on implementing new TEL systems at Dell.

In addition to the infrastructure, hardware, software, legal, IT, and process issues associated with implementing TEL solutions at Dell, there is a more fundamental barrier that we are combating as well: i.e., the classroom learning barrier. Most people have been sent to class to learn in elementary school, high school, college, and in graduate schools. The most comfortable way to learn is to sit in a room and have someone "pour" the learning into the participants. The learning has been very prescriptive and pre-formulated. A student in a traditional classroom doesn't really have to think about how to learn; he or she only has to think about how to exercise short-term memory, so that the follow-on assessment can be passed. So, when a major initiative is launched to get people to learn in a self-directed fashion, it seems painful. It doesn't seem like learning or training. It is one of the biggest issues we will face as we try to facilitate more self-directed learning at Dell.

Purpose

This document will be used to clearly delineate the benefits, challenges, risks, requirements, and direction for TEL at Dell.

Let's look at overall benefits for the use of TEL solutions at Dell. These are broken down into two major categories.

Benefits for the Learner

There are a variety of benefits to the learner at Dell who uses TEL solutions. Here are samples of them:

Increased learner control. The learner can control a variety of factors associated with the learning process. He or she can access the learning at a variety of times. He or she can navigate through the learning in a non-linear fashion if desired. If adequate feedback and assessments are provided in the tool, the learner can bypass unnecessary or redundant knowledge or skills.

Quicker access to learning. When a traditional classroom-based learning event is implemented, the participants are held hostage to the space resources available. For example, if a new software application is to be rolled out across the enterprise and it was necessary for 5,000 people to get trained on it in the classroom, it is obvious that there would quickly be a backlog waiting for available PC lab or classroom space. However, a TEL solution (if implemented appropriately) could be driven across the organization much quicker.

Performance support tools. Many TEL solutions can be used inherently as performance support when the learning is completed. There are many technology-based learning solutions that actually can be used as part of the on-the-job performance support.

Reduced time away from the job. Every hour spent in the classroom increases the opportunity costs associated with job incumbents being away from their workspaces. Additionally, travel time to and from the classroom is nonproductive. When personnel can take training from their desktops or on the shop floor or on their portables, they can stay connected to the job.

Process-based learning vs. event-based learning. Some TEL can be used in small chunks, when needed, over a period of time to help ensure that the information is learned. Most classroom-based learning is event-driven. The learning is compressed into a bundle of time, e.g., four hours, eight hours, sixteen hours, etc. Learning never takes an odd amount of time in the classroom. It's always complete on the hour.

More learning interventions available. When TEL solutions are used, there can be a greater variety of learning solutions available. Because personnel don't have to "wait" until an instructor and class are available, more interventions are available.

Benefits for Dell Computer Corporation

Reduced cost. Dell Computer Corporation can save a tremendous amount of money, opportunity cost, and travel-related expense by using TEL solutions.

Reduced time. There can be a tremendous amount of time compression from the classroom when TEL solutions are used. Compression of up to 65 percent is possible using technology. This has already been demonstrated at Dell in many instances with interventions such as New Hire Orientation, New Hire Sales Training, and On-Line Legal Briefings.

Greater impact in the beginning. Because a TEL solution can be implemented to a large audience simultaneously, impact of a learning solution can be greater...quicker. Contrast this with a classroom-based course that must be delivered over periods of months or years to reach the target audience.

Risks Associated with Movement towards Technology-Enabled Learning

There are some risks associated with the use of TEL solutions at Dell. Here are some of them:

Infrastructure issues can slow down implementation. Dell's IT infrastructure requirements are complex and unique. Most products that can be bought "off the shelf" can't be readily integrated into Dell's IT system. Every new *production* application must go through a thorough Software Development Lifecycle (SDLC) process to get fully supported by Dell IT. This means that most things cannot be requested today and implemented next week. It's not realistic or prudent to force things through the process. Lack of IT support is risky.

Taking shortcuts is risky. Although it may seem like the right thing to do, taking shortcuts and bypassing key steps in the SDLC process is ultimately risky. Nonproduction servers (known as *rogue servers*) are not supported by IT and can be shut down at any time.

Acute change is more difficult for people to accept than incremental change. People don't like acute change. Acute change happens when things change very rapidly. This is especially true when the changed activity or operation or procedure is also more difficult (or perceived to be more difficult) than the previous way of doing things. People have been learning the same way for hundreds of years and to cause acute change in the learning arena can prove detrimental. It is important to analyze the potential impact of changing the learning landscape too rapidly, before people are ready to change. Once a person is dissatisfied with learning in a new way, it is hard to get them to engage in a similar vein in the future. It is more appropriate to look for ways to facilitate incremental change, i.e., change that occurs over a longer period of time in phases.

Hardware and software longevity (or brevity) can be expensive. Hardware and software advances are occurring daily in today's society. Today's must-have technology is tomorrow's ancient history. Accordingly, decisions cannot be made too lightly about technology choices. Cost-benefit analyses should be applied to any TEL buying opportunity.

New model requires new skill sets. The new learning model which will lend itself heavily to alternative-learning-based and TEL solutions will require new skill sets in the learning development, implementation, and maintenance phases. Just as a skilled subject matter expert can't necessarily facilitate learning well, the traditional classroom-based instructor may not have skills that transcend into the field of TEL solutions. Taking content from a classroom and converting it to text for the computer monitor is not creating TEL.

Communication is key. Successful programs of any kind have sound communication as a common thread. Upcoming learning events, current learning opportunities, and past successes should be regularly and consistently communicated up and down the entire organization. It is important that the end users of the TEL solutions also have simple to use feedback loops to allow communication about changes in the content and/or methods used.

Policies and Guidelines

As with any major initiative, there should be policies and guidelines in place. One set of overarching principles that should be considered in any new TEL solution implementation is the formula for Dell Learning (DL).

$$DL = Learning + Access + Technology + Leverage - Cost - Time - Touches$$

Any solution that is brought into the enterprise should strive to increase access, the use of technology, and leverage across the organization, and cost less, take less time, and take less touches to implement. If not, another solution(s) should be considered.

Policies and guidelines will need to be established by the VP of Dell Learning, the Dell Learning Technology Services Team, the Senior Staff of Dell Learning, and also other key stakeholder organizations at Dell including IT, Legal, Global Information Protection, HRIM, and others as necessary, based on the TEL strategy.

Current Successes

In determining any operational strategy, it is beneficial to take a look at the current landscape and see what types of projects, activities, relationships, and solutions have been successful. An analysis of these successes can identify common threads of excellence and best practice that can be used in future implementation of TEL projects.

Relationship building with stakeholders. In the past, when Dell Learning has wanted to implement a new learning technology, we asked for support from IT, an appropriate amount of noise was made in support of us, and in the end we would have to build things ourselves. Since software engineering and development of detailed Functional Requirements Specifications (FRS) has never been a core competence of Dell Learning, we made many mistakes in the implementation of learning technologies. Since the DLTS team has been formed, better relationships have been established with IT, HRIM, HRSM, Dell Intractive, Legal, and Global Information Protection (GIP). Many members of Dell Learning Corporate (and now many regional training groups) have IT involved as early as the conception of a solution to help ensure that all infrastructure, hardware, software, and security issues are addressed prior to starting a new TEL project. Several members of the HRIM and HRSM teams routinely attend the DLTS staff meeting biweekly. These improved communications and relationships are helping to ensure the success of new TEL projects.

Star Trainer from Simtrex. How do you train many new sales reps on DOMS using real phones and simulated order entry software around the clock if necessary? With Star Trainer. This call center simulation tool being implemented by HSB training with assistance from DLTS, Procurement, Finance, HRIT, and others is a great example of a cross-functional effort to implement a new learning technology. The team has worked together to provide input in areas of expertise where necessary from helping to establish initial requirements, identifying functional requirements, a thorough cost-benefit analysis, contracting (including capitalization of equipment and software), parallel piloting and development, etc. The HSB team is already looking at ways to leverage this technology across other sales organizations and into other call center environments.

Video Visor from Digital Lava. If you'd like to have thirty frames per second video digitized on CD and linked to PowerPoint slides, web pages, applications, pictures, and other files with search capability and subtitles, then Video Visor is the way to go. In addition to a tremendous amount of functionality, production costs (a very affordable service level agreement was negotiated) and time are minimal, and people who have seen or used it to date are begging for more. It's been used to date for Enterprise Selling in the Relationship group, the Regional Executive Forum, and for a distance learning effort with Dell New Zealand.

Strategy

The following questions need to be answered in order to get a firm grasp of the direction that Dell Learning needs to take as it pursues more and more TEL solutions.

What do we need to track, measure, and report on?

An organization must be able to track, measure, and report on a variety of data in order to ensure that TEL solutions are being used appropriately. Here are a sample selection of data that should be captured to assess the effectiveness of TEL solutions in an organization:

1. Identity of people taking training, including badge number, manager name, business segment, and job title, at a minimum.
2. Length of time spent in a TEL solution and times that TEL are used.
3. Navigation while using a TEL solution. Also how people are getting to TEL offerings.
4. Chargeback data, including cost center information and course cost.
5. Assessment results.
6. User sessions for those TEL that are web-based.
7. Usage metrics for all other types of TEL.
8. Freshness dates of all content and/or web sites used for learning. Also need to identify content owners for all content.
9. Rollup reporting for all TEL courses by manager, job title, business segment, function, and overall.

What is best taught with technology?

Not all knowledge, skills, or attitudes can or should be taught with any one medium or method. Technology should be used where it has an advantage to bear when implemented. It should *never* be implemented for the sake of using technology. Technology is a tool or a medium, not the message. Here are some things that technology is good for:

Teaching people to know. Technology is a great way to help people get information they need quickly. Look at the stock market… its existence hinges on information. The better and more timely the information, the better the stakeholders' (and stockholders') decisions. Think about a stock market that had to share information by word of mouth, in classrooms. It would be unthinkable. The markets would probably suffer as well as the stakeholders and stockholders in the market. So, technology is a great tool to share information or knowledge with a great number of people at the same time in many locations.

Preparing people to do. There are times when you want participants to come into a classroom or a lab or an orientation ready to get right into the skills practice. Maybe they are going to practice sales negotiations or practice coaching or learn how to drive a golf ball off the tee. One great way to facilitate this is to provide a TEL tool that allows the participant to get background information before the skill practice. This could be in the form of a web site, or a CD ROM, or maybe participation in a threaded discussion before the actual classroom session.

Creating a large impact quickly. If the federal government makes an official announcement restricting travel to a country where many people in the company might travel, what's the best way to get this information out quickly? It's not in the classroom. Emails could be sent out or emails with URLs imbedded in them. Alternatively, web casts can be done with the important message on it. If you need to get information out to a large number of people quickly, technology is the way to go.

What is best taught with more traditional methods?

There are certain knowledge, skills, and attitudes that are best taught with more traditional methods, including classroom and other forms of directed learning. Here are some examples:

Teaching people to do. There are a myriad of skill-based learning opportunities that are much easier to get in the classroom or in the work environment. How difficult is it to teach someone to make a presentation using technology? How does someone get to act as a sales team member interfacing with a computer screen? So, when we are trying to get people to practice skills (other than those that implicitly require the use of technology, e.g., a new software application) then the effort, cost, and resources required to use technology may be prohibitive. If people need immediate feedback on task completion or demonstration, it can generally be handled more easily in the classroom or on the job site with an instructor.

Facilitating relationship building in individuals, groups, and teams. If you want people to work together because of the jobs they have or to instill new potential networks, the classroom and other social learning settings can help this effort. People are often more communicative with other people when they have met them face to face the first time.

Reinforcing learning on a regular basis. Most learning that occurs with the use of TEL doesn't have a strong feedback and reinforcement system associated with it. Knowledgeable peers and managers can help employees continue to use and build on skills with quick on-the-job sessions, lunch and learns, staff meeting updates, and other opportunities.

What will we accommodate? What will we change?

There are several issues that are important to consider as we migrate towards the use of more and more TEL solutions.

Constraints and limitations. Dell Learning wants to use technology to leverage learning across the enterprise. Many of the applications/systems that we want to use require a large amount of network bandwidth, require dedicated servers and support, and sometimes don't fit within the current breadth of IT supported systems. To move forward with some of the desired technology will require an enterprise-wide support of investment in necessary hardware, software, and network technology. In the interim, Dell Learning will continue to push the envelope on what we can bring in, in the hopes of driving change in baseline computer configurations, etc.

Paradigm changes of learners. Even if we have all of the hardware and technology constraints resolved, there will still be an issue of user acceptance of the new technology. This will be an issue that we will grapple with incessantly over the next year(s). The key is to know that this problem exists and will continue to exist until our clients feel satisfied about these offerings as actual learning systems that will work.

What standards and/or guidelines will be used to govern implementation of new TEL solutions?

At a basic level it is imperative that all new TEL solutions meet the IT production requirements for applications. They must be compliant with IT requirements so that they can be on production servers in the server farm and thus supported by IT and the Client Assistance Center (CAC). Additionally, they must be in compliance with GIP and other security requirements and legal compliance. Appropriate licensing (either to the desktop or across the enterprise) must be in place to ensure that we are using applications and software appropriately. When possible, applications should be able to sit on a server with other applications. New applications must be Y2K certifiable. An application project team consisting of Dell Learning, HRIT, HRSM, GIP, Procurement, Legal, Business Partners, Vendors, and other necessary personnel should guide the new application through the SDLC process until the application is in production.

A cost-benefit analysis should be conducted to determine if the new application will cost more to implement than the benefit will be.

Any new projects that are initiated from Dell Learning must be sanctioned as actual IT-supported projects or we run the risk of nonsupport from the IT organization.

What baseline technology must we have?

The baseline technology we will need in the upcoming year(s) includes:

- Threaded Discussion tools
- Internet Paging tools like Internet Messenger from Microsoft
- Knowledge Management System
- Video Streaming Capabilities and Video Servers
- Robust Management and Tracking System for Online Learning
- Virtual Service Representatives (chatterbots)
- Best Practices Database

What will it take to manage this?

As with any function, data gathering and analysis is key to the successful management of an operation or function. In addition to the need for data management, there will be other resources required to make this migration to TEL successful.

How will online learning be managed?

Online learning at its most base level will need to be analyzed, designed, developed, implemented, and evaluated by a set of dedicated resource people. This team also needs a robust tracking system, quality assurance processes, and technical support of various stakeholder organizations within Dell. The following areas should be managed:

- Research of new technologies
- New TEL solution implementation and planning for maintenance
- Tracking and reporting of usage and effectiveness
- Fiscal operations
- Quality assurance including automated ways to help ensure content is fresh
- ROI data
- Customer education about TEL

What will it take for the learner to manage it?

The learner has some other considerations to help manage his or her learning. The learner needs the following:

- Ready access to the learning
- Support from direct and higher-level management
- Education about how to use TEL
- Self-efficacy training and/or communication
- Opportunity to practice and make mistakes
- Tracking system
- Feedback system for TEL
- A roadmap for TEL so that the learner can see where to go and how to get there

What are the marketing/communication issues around the use of technology to enable learning?

There are no switches that can be flipped to erase the hundreds and thousands of years of centralized social learning models that we have all been immersed in from early childhood. For this reason, and more so than with other traditional learning opportunities, a strong communication effort must be made to communicate benefits, motivational information, and other information that will help the learner feel at ease with TEL solutions. There have been TEL solutions implemented that have not been as effective as they could have been, and in a sense, people that have had these experiences have to get pulled back into the fold.

It is important that successes are communicated early and often in this area and that people are well aware of any upcoming new TEL to be released and how it will benefit them. It is also important that changes made to TEL solutions based on user feedback be communicated appropriately with end users so that they feel we are making business-based decisions to adjust solutions as appropriate. This helps increase the likelihood of people providing valuable feedback to us about TEL effectiveness.

A marketing person should have at least partial responsibility for this effort.

Who do we have to partner with?

In order for us to succeed in the TEL arena, there are many key people we need to establish and maintain relationships with, including:

- IT
- HRIT
- HRSM
- GIP
- Legal
- Procurement
- DLTS
- Business Unit IT organizations (including global partners)
- Business Partner Subject Matter Experts (including global SMEs)
- Qualified Vendors
- Strategic Partners using TEL

Summary

Offering TEL solutions with all of the course offerings is the right thing to do for Dell and for our intended audiences. The use of TEL provides a variety of course offerings and learning opportunities, it creates greater impact quicker, it allows flexibility in offerings, and it empowers the learner.

However, there are many challenges associated with the appropriate implementation of TEL at Dell. There are cultural and learning style issues; there are infrastructure, hardware, software, system, and network constraints. And there is the tremendous issue of getting people comfortable with this emerging use of technology.

This paper is designed to establish a framework for a TEL strategy at Dell. It is meant to be a living document that will evolve as Dell's TEL environment changes.

Learning Byte   *Does everyone learn the same way? No. So, it's a good idea to offer several flavors of a learning solution so that each person's learning preference is addressed. Alternatively, incorporate several learning methods in each solution so that it is cross-functional.*

Glossary

CAC - Client Assistance Center (AKA 8-4040)

CER - Construction Exit Review, this is the closeout meeting in the SDLC process.

DLS – Dell Learning Solutions, a corporate learning organization that has a team of performance consultants that provide consulting services to the business units.

DLTS – Dell Learning Technology Services, a corporate learning organization dedicated to implementing new learning technology across the Dell enterprise.

FER – Functional Exit Review, the kick-off meeting for the SDLC process. This is where the functional requirements are clearly identified and discussed.

GIP – Global Information Protection, this is the group that provides security for all of Dell's information and applications.

HRIM - Human Resources Information Management

HRSM – Human Resources Systems Management

SDLC – Software Development Lifecycle Process

TEL - Technology Enabled Learning

Y2K Testing – Testing required to ensure that a new application will meet Y2K test criteria. Test scripts are written for the application that include a series of critical Y2K dates to ensure that the application remains stable.

Functional Requirements Specification Template

This section of the strategy can be used for any resources that need to be included.

A Functional Requirements Specification Template
When you are going to buy or build a new learning application (especially those that are technology-enabled) it is important that you thoroughly identify *the functional requirements* of the new solution. If you clearly identify what your functional requirements are for the solution you need, you can much more easily locate the vendor or end-solution. It will also help you to cull out those vendors or solutions that may not be the most appropriate for your needs. Use this template to identify the functional requirements of the solution you need.

Introduction
- *Purpose of the document* — Use this section to state the purpose of the Functional Requirements document. Identify how it will and won't be used.
- *System scope*— Identify the scope of the system that will be defined in the document. Identify systems and subsystems that will be included and those that won't be included as a part of the system.
- *Definitions, acronyms, and abbreviations* — Define words that need to be defined. Identify acronyms and abbreviations that are used.
- *References* — Identify any references, procedures, or other documents that were used to create the document. These may be used again to research questions that arise.
- *Overview of the document* — Provide a high-level summary of the document including identification of major sections. An outline format is useful and facilitates organization of the information.

General Description

- *Product perspective* — Describe the overall functionality of the product. What is the product intended to do? What is the product not supposed to do?
- *Overview of functional requirements* — What are the high-level functional requirements? What must this product be able to do? What is not acceptable?
- *Overview of system properties* — What properties does the system need? What properties will not be allowed?
- *Compatibility* — What systems and applications will this new system have to interface with? Are there infrastructure systems and/or legacy systems that the new application must integrate with? Are there database systems or other back end systems that can or can't be used? Will the application have to sit on its own server or can it share space with other applications on a server? (This is an important consideration unless you want to buy a new server for each new application you create.)
- *Overview of constraints* — Are there bandwidth restrictions? What software, applications, or systems can't be used? When does your organization need the application installed? What limitations are there on development and application costs? Will the system operate locally, interstate, or globally? Will the application reside inside the firewall or will it sit on an external server? Who will have access to the application? Who will be allowed to administer the application? Will modifications be allowed to be made on the system? If so, who can make them? Who owns the application? What license requirements are there? How can the application be distributed? How can't it be distributed?
- *User characteristics* — What types of personnel will be using the application? Where will people be using the application? How experienced are people using the application? What limitations do end users have where they will be using the systems (e.g., low lighting, limited access to systems, need for touch screens, etc.)?
- *Operational environment* — What is the environment like where the system will be used? Are there desktop systems or terminals available for personnel to use? Are folks using portables with docking stations? Do people use kiosks? What types of software are used across the enterprise?

- *Goals and non-goals* — What is/are the reason(s) that the new application is being used? What shouldn't it be used for?
- *Assumptions and dependencies* — State all of assumptions and dependencies to get the system implemented.

Specific Requirements
- *Interfaces* — What types of systems, hardware, and other applications does the new system have to interface with? What legacy systems does this need to interface with? What is the graphical user interface (GUI) and how will it work?
- *System properties* — Identify the system properties that you will have to consider in the implementation of the new application. Will it ultimately reside on the desktop? Will it have to be used over a local area network or other network? What operating system is used for it?
- *Constraints* — List any constraints associated with implementation of the system including:

  - *Real Time* — Does the application have to respond in real time? Or is it okay that the information input is static unless updated manually?
  - *Security* — What security requirements does your organization have? Who should be able to access the application? Who shouldn't be able to access the application? Will the application be accessible outside of the organization's firewall? If so, what kind of content will be allowed?
  - *Fault management* — How is the system protected? What happens if the application crashes? How will the application be recovered? How often does the application or data supporting the application need to be backed up? Who can make administrative changes to the system? Where will the application reside?
  - *Configurability* — What company standards are there for application configuration? What other applications does the application have to interact with?
  - *Administration* — Who will administer the tool when it is in production? How will the tool be administered? How many people will be needed to administer the system effectively?

♦ *Hardware* — What hardware will be required to run the application? Who will have to buy the hardware? Who is responsible for set up of servers and other hardware that will be required to get the application operational initially? Does the application have to be on a stand-alone server or can it share space on an application server?

Development Requirements

- *Build environment* — What type of environment can the application be built in?
- *Tools* — What tools are authorized for use by your organization to develop new applications? Are there tools that you are specifically prohibited from using?
- *Hardware* — What hardware has been designated as developmental hardware? What limitations are there on developmental hardware? What does the IT organization allow developers to do in the developmental environment and on developmental servers?
- *Software* — What software has been designated as developmental software? Are there specific developmental software tools that cannot be used or aren't supported by the IT organization?

Deferred Features

- *Deferred features* — Deferred features are features in the application that don't have to be rolled out in the initial release of the application. Some new applications require input from other applications and systems that may not be ready to go for the overall functionality of the application. Does this mean that the business will allow the application rollout to be delayed indefinitely because full functionality will not be there in the initial release? Probably not. So a way to avoid this scenario is to implement various levels of functionality in phases. Implement the most business critical functionality first and then add on to it as possible and appropriate.
- *Explicit restrictions* — Are there absolute restrictions or constraints that will make or break the application project? Is there a dollar

amount that will be considered excessive? Is there an operating system that is expressly forbidden to be used? Can vendors implement the application or does it have to be done completely in-house? Are there time requirements that are restrictive? Does the application have to be implemented by a certain date? The latter part of 1999 this issue came up with the Y2K problem. Many companies implemented moratoriums on new application development/implementation in the last quarter of the year in an effort to be responsive to Y2K emergencies that might emerge and also to minimize the impact of potential problems with existing business-critical applications. Are there restrictions on types of software, file size or type, or other restrictions that apply?

QA

- *Criteria/metrics* — What criteria will be used to help measure what constitutes a successful implementation of the project? How will all parties know the project is actually completed and in a maintenance stage? What metrics will be used to measure success? Who will actually gather the data, create reports, and make recommendations on quality of the product when it is in production? What incentives and processes are in place to help ensure that the application will actually be maintained appropriately?
- *Unit tests* — What tests will be completed on units to verify satisfactory operation? How many systems will be tested and what tests will be conducted? Who will conduct the tests? Who has to sign off on completion of the tests? How often do the tests have to be conducted?
- *Reference to QA test plan* — Who will validate that the tests are conducted in accordance with the QA test plan? How often will the test plan be implemented?

Documentation

- *New manuals required* — Will new documentation or manuals be required for the end-user population? What training will be needed for the end users to facilitate use of the new application? Who will develop the documentation? Who will maintain the documentation? Who will conduct the end-user training? Will online documentation be used? If so, does it mitigate the need for paper-based manuals?

- *Manuals requiring modification* — Are there existing manuals that will require revisions or removal from the enterprise? How will the manuals be modified? Who will modify the manuals? Will modified manuals be online or paper-based?

Appendix A *Initial list of risks/issues* — In any new project there are inherent risks and/or issues. In the rush to meet business needs and to drive projects to completion, project managers and team members often skip the very necessary step of identifying and documenting risks and issues in the very beginning of a project. Many of the risks are inconsequential. However, each project can have several major risks associated with it. Risks by themselves are not a problem. Undocumented risks that haven't been agreed upon by the project manager and the client/sponsors can be detrimental and downright ugly. If a business critical process is hindered or a timeline is delayed, the domino effect on interrelated systems can debilitate an enterprise. If these risks are noted in the beginning and agreed to by key parties, all parties share in the risk equally... and openly. Take the time to document these as soon as possible. If necessary, periodically review and update the list of risks and get agreement as needed.

Appendix B *Design Notes* — Identify any notes or functional requirements and/or design requirements for the product to be developed.

Appendix C *Bibliography*

Web Sites

- **www.learn2now.com** — The author's web site for ongoing best practices and learning discussions in the on-demand learning arena. Send questions and comments to the author and join in a threaded conversation. This will be the incubator for future ideas and sharing.

- **http://www.trainingsupersite.com/publications/newsletters/ tfl/tfl_toc.htm** — *Technology for Learning Site* — The tagline on this site is "Practical ideas for creating a wired, retooled, and networked learning organization." Register for a free copy of the newsletter. If you like it... subscribe.

- **http://www.trainingsupersite.com/tss_link/lakeset.htm** — *TRAINING* Magazine online.

- **www.brandon-hall.com** — Brandon Hall has an excellent web site with a tremendous amount of information on web-based and online learning experiences. See his most recent papers, articles, and studies and send notes to the author, too.

- **http://www.ittrain.com/** — *Inside Technology Training Magazine*. A great magazine that focuses on the use of technology and learning. Subscriptions are free after completing a subscription qualification form.

- **www.neuromedia.com** — Go to see a chatterbot in action and to see a chatterbot development engine.

- **www.hrdpress.com** — An online resource for manager's pocket guides and assessments.

- **www.corpu.com** — Corporate University Exchange™ has a web site to discuss corporate university learning issues and to publicize upcoming learning events and discussions.

- **www.theinternetmap.com** — Go to learn about (and order) the Internet Map.

- **www.ninthhouse.com** — Discover how Ninth House web-based learning works and see sample videos. If you like what you see, you can subscribe online.

- **www.caemedia.com/** — See how CAE Media uses the DigiCard. Get information about development requirements, costs, and specifications.

- **www.salesmaker.com** — Discover how to use sales-based audio learning materials.

- **www.flipcards.com** — This site contains information on off-the-shelf and custom flipcards for computers.

- **http://www.wfs.org/** — The World Future Society is a nonprofit educational and scientific organization for people interested in how social and technological developments are shaping the future. With 30,000 members, the Society serves as a nonpartisan clearinghouse for ideas about the future, including forecasts, recommendations, scenarios, alternatives, and more.

- **www.masie.com** — Home of the Masie Center's web site (*The Technology & Learning Thinktank*). Get information on the Masie Center, read about services they offer, research articles, join the Masie Center, buy books from the Techlearn Bookstore, or register for an upcoming conference.

- **www.dictionary.com** — I recommend you bookmark this site and have it readily available to look up words.

- **www.techweb.com** — Tech Web site for IT professionals. Great information, e-zines, and a fantastic encyclopedia.

Magazines

→ *Inside Technology Training*, Ziff-Davis Professional Publishing Group
— published monthly except August and December
→ *Fast Company Magazine*

Company Contact Information

CAE Media
500 West Wood Street
Palantine, IL 60067
Tel: (800) 627-0033
Fax: (847) 991-3385

Digital Lava Inc.
13160 Mindanao Way
Suite 350
Marina del Rey, CA 90292
Tel: (310) 577-0200
Fax: (310) 306-3373

Left Coast Interactive
401-F Miller Ave.
Mill Valley, CA 94941
Tel: (415) 389-1599
Fax: (415) 389-1699

The InternetMap Company
25 Highland Park Village
Suite 100-380
Dallas, TX 75205
Tel: (214) 742-6700

The Limited, Inc.
Three Limited Parkway
Columbus, OH 43230

Training Administration Systems

There are a variety of Training Administrations available for training organizations to use to track and manage their training resources and delivery. But, these are not the only systems that are available. This section provides a snapshot of some available systems. This information comes from a report completed by Tobin-Erdmann & Jacobsen and is reprinted with their permission.

This section includes company descriptions for developers/suppliers of the following software:

- Manager's Edge — Allen Communication
- Pathware 4 — Lotus
- Profis — Networks North
- Phoenix — Pathlore Software Corporation
- Pinnacle Learning Manager — Pinnacle Multimedia
- Plateau 2.0 — Plateau Systems Ltd.
- Education Management System — Saba Software
- TrainingServer 3.1 — Syscom
- Training Management Software — HRD Press

Manager's Edge

Allen Communication
5 Triad Center, 5th Floor
Salt Lake City, UT 84180
USA
Tel: (801) 537-7800
Toll Free: (800) 325-7850
Technical Support: (800) 515-2626
Fax: (801) 537-7805
Email: info@allencomm.com

http://www.allencomm.com/about/

About Allen Communication

Allen Communication is in the business of teaching and training via computer and interactive multimedia technology. Allen introduced the first commercial interactive videodisc in 1981. For several years after, many interactive video-training programs were created on the Allen System. The company provides instructional support courseware, hardware, and software. Allen is both a software and courseware development company.

Allen Communication products include: Designer's Edge®, a revolutionary planning and pre-authoring tool; Trainer's Edge™; The Quest Multimedia Authoring System®; Manager's Edge™, to help organize online curriculum and collect critical student performance data from a single location; and CBT Developer Suite™, for a more robust performance tracking system.

Allen Communication's products reflect a firsthand understanding of the multimedia development process, which the company has gained through eighteen years of developing custom multimedia training courses.

In 1994, Allen Communication was acquired by Times Mirror, a large media and information company. This acquisition has allowed Allen Communication to use its multimedia expertise to enhance the offerings of all of Times Mirror's companies, which fall into the three divisions of print media, professional information, and consumer media. Times Mirror also owns AchieveGlobal, the world's largest soft skills company.

Pathware 4

Lotus Corporate Offices

Lotus Development Corporation
55 Cambridge Parkway
Cambridge, MA 02142 USA
Tel: (617) 577-8500

http://www.lotus.com/home.nsf

Lotus/Macromedia
Macromedia, Incorporated
600 Townsend Street
San Francisco, CA 94103
Tel: (415) 252-2000
Fax: (415) 626-0554

http://www.macromedia.com/macromedia/

About Lotus:

Founded: 1982 by Mitch Kapor and Jonathan Sachs
Employees: Currently 8,000 worldwide
Worldwide: Marketing products in 80 countries
Business Partners: Over 18,000 worldwide
Acquired by IBM: Late spring of 1995
Lotus firsts: On-screen help system tutorial on floppy PC customer
support program

Press Release:

**MACROMEDIA AND LOTUS DEVELOPMENT ENTER STRATEGIC
PARTNERSHIP TO BRING WEB-BASED LEARNING INTO THE
MAINSTREAM**

*IBM's Lotus to Purchase Macromedia Pathware Business; Companies to Jointly
Develop, Market and Distribute Technologies for Web-based Learning*

San Francisco, Calif. and Cambridge, Mass.—July 29, 1999—
Macromedia Inc. and IBM's Lotus Development Corp. today announced
an agreement that will expand the market for Web-based learning and
create the industry's most comprehensive online teaching and learning
solutions. The new offerings will give businesses, schools, and other
organizations a simple means of creating, delivering, tracking, and
managing Web-based training and coursework.

Under the agreement, Lotus will purchase the Macromedia Pathware
business and distribute certain other of Macromedia's authoring software
for Web-based learning. Pathware is Macromedia's market-leading
learning management system. The Macromedia group that develops and
markets Pathware will become part of Lotus' Distributed Learning
Business Group, which develops and markets Lotus LearningSpace, the
company's Web-based distributed learning platform. Macromedia will
continue to ship, sell, and support Pathware until a transition to the Lotus
Distributed Learning Division is completed. Lotus will then sell and
support Pathware as a stand-alone product.

Profis

Network's North

NTN Interactive Network Inc.
14 Meteor Drive
Etobicoke, Ontario, M9W 1A4
Canada
Tel: (416) 675-6666
Fax: (416) 675-8838
Toll Free: (800) 661-PLAY (7529)

http://www.ntnc.com

About NTN:

Networks North Inc., is a public company with many years' experience in educational media, interactive television, and Internet solutions. With 110 employees and offices in Vancouver, Toronto, Saint John, and Atlanta, Networks North business units have over twenty-five years' experience in delivering video and interactive media to educational, government, and corporate markets. The company, through its 100 percent–owned subsidiary Interlynx Multimedia Inc., has developed PROFIS, a leading edge software solution for companies seeking to place interactive learning materials and courseware on the Internet or on a corporate market.

Phoenix

Pathlore Software Corporation
Corporate Headquarters
7965 North High Street, Suite 300
Columbus, OH 43235
Tel: (888) PATHLORE (728-4567)
Tel: (614) 781-0036
Fax: (614) 781-7200

112 South Alfred Street, Suite 350
Alexandria, VA 22314

Tel: (703) 684-3970
Fax: (703) 684-3968

http://www.pathlore.co.uk

About Pathlore:

Headquartered in Columbus, Ohio, Pathlore is a provider of computer-based training solutions. More than 80 percent of banks with assets greater than $3 billion and 70 percent of Fortune 1000 companies rely on Pathlore solutions to train their workforces. Pathlore Software Corporation is a privately held company whose focus is to deliver complete solutions for enterprise-wide, results-driven training to corporations worldwide.

Pathlore has been delivering enterprise CBT solutions since 1978. Indeed, Pathlore's core product, PHOENIX, set the standard for enterprise CBT.

Pathlore has grown rapidly since its divestiture from Legent Corp. in November 1995. Pathlore now:

- distributes products in forty countries, including the U.S.
- receives more than 24 percent of its revenue from international sales
- has opened three offices overseas
- has increased its number of employees from 25 to more than 100 since November 1995

Pathlore's PHOENIX® delivers "virtual classroom" solutions across corporate networks, intranets, and the Internet. Pathlore also provides Professional Services consulting for instructional design, course development, and IT integration.

Pinnacle Learning Manager

Pinnacle Multimedia
12637 South 265 West #300
P. O. Box 1409
Draper, UT 84020-1409
Toll Free: (800) 738-9800
Tel: (801) 523-8000
Fax: (801) 523-8012

http://www.courseware.com/

About Pinnacle:
Incorporated in 1992, Pinnacle Multimedia produces comprehensive training management software. Its flagship product, the Pinnacle Learning Manager™ (PLM), enables trainers to connect with various computer courseware, and manages the data with one central database.

Plateau 2.0

Plateau Systems, Ltd.
4041 University Drive, Suite 400
Fairfax, VA 22030
Fax: (703) 934-1363

http://www.plateausystems.com

About Plateau:
Plateau Systems, Ltd., is located in Fairfax, Virginia. Plateau specializes in the development, implementation, and integration of systems to manage training and related data. Plateau products are in service at over 200 companies in the United States and abroad. Plateau Systems offers custom software development services to meet a customer's special training requirements. This development may include the development of custom reports, specialized data entry windows, additional functionality, or other unique features.

Education Management System

Saba Software, Inc.
2400 Bridge Parkway
Redwood Shores, CA 94065-1166
Tel: (650) 696-3840
Fax: (650) 696-1773

http://www.Sabasoftware.com/

About Saba:
Saba's mission is to help businesses improve their results by providing a learning management solution that aligns people's learning with their business. The core values Saba espouses are:

- Foster enduring relationships with customers, partners, and employees
- Respect, empower, and energize people
- Create value through continuous innovation, change, and accomplishment
- Manage truthfully and responsibly

Saba's global customers serve more than 1.5 million people around the world. Announced customers include: Baan, Ceridian, Documentum, Netscape, and Wells Fargo. Saba's growing list of partners includes industry-leading learning content developers, service providers, management consultants, enterprise applications vendors, and technology suppliers. A sampling includes AchieveGlobal, Baan, Bell Canada Enterprises Media Division, Catapult (an IBM subsidiary), Deloitte and Touche, DigitalThink, Interpersonal Technology Group, Microsoft, MindQ Publishing (a Knowledge Universe company), NetG, Netscape, Oracle, PeopleSciences, SAP, SkillScape, and TECH Connect.

The *Saba Education Management System*™ is the award-winning Internet learning management system for the extended enterprise. Brandon Hall Resources named the *Saba Education Management System* the "Best Enterprise-Wide Training Management System" in a 1998 report that analyzed over sixty systems, and The Masie Center designated it as the only "World-Wide Enterprise-Wide Training Management System" in a 1998 online publication.

Products include *Saba Competency Manager*™, *Saba LearningOnline*™, *Saba Financials Connections*™, *Saba HR Connections*™, and *Saba eCommerce Connections*™ and a full range of management consulting, business process reengineering, technical implementation consulting, education, and support services.

TrainingServer 3.1

Syscom, Inc.
400 East Pratt Street
Suite 200
Baltimore, MD 21202
Tel: (800) 7-SYSCOM

http://www.syscom-inc.com

About Syscom:

SYSCOM's mission has been to excel in specific niche software services and product markets. It has evolved into a growing company of divisions directed to develop these market niches. SYSCOM was founded in 1982 by Ted Bayer, a native of Baltimore. Early projects included the design of large-scale databases and the custom development of unique system utilities for supporting large, around-the-clock, database systems.

SYSCOM designed the first successful automated hierarchical to relational data propagation bridge for IBM to the contractual services industry. With over 200 employees, annual revenues have increased by an average of over 80 percent, to $33 million in 1998. SYSCOM currently provides specialized, comprehensive, information technology services and products for large organizations, both public and private, from Tokyo to London. Current major areas of business include state human resources systems support services, systems integration of workflow and document management systems, complete project life-cycle software support services, and training and qualification management software.

Since its inception in 1992, SYSCOM's TrainingServer has consistently been the most advanced training administration software offering available. Citibank, MCI, the U.S. Strategic Air Command, and many others use TrainingServer in support of enterprise-wide training. Through its companion products it continues to be the industry leader in the use of telephony with TrainingTeleserver and Internet technologies with TrainingServer@Online, as well as providing the latest in business functionality for administering corporate training.

Training Management Software

HRD Press
22 Amherst Road
Amherst, MA 01002
Tel: (800) 822-2801

http://www.hrdpress.com

Training Management Software is a cost-effective solution for tracking employee training. Network and Internet versions are available.

Glossary

Asynchronous Learning — In online learning, an event in which people are not logged on at the same time. For example, the instructor might publish a lecture on a web site and learners would read it when their schedules permit (Carliner, p. 105). Contrast with *Synchronous Learning*.

CBT — Computer-Based Training — Using the computer for training and instruction. CBT programs are called "courseware" and provide interactive training sessions for all disciplines. CBT uses graphics extensively, as well as CD-ROM and LaserDisc. (www.techweb.com)

Chatterbot — Web-based bots that are designed to communicate with the end user by responding to key terms or patterns that the bot reads. See www.neuromedia.com for an example bot.

Configured Work — "Work that is defined and designed in place, in response to the situation at hand, and by the person(s) doing it" (Nickols). *See also Prefigured Work.*

Fading — The gradual removal of the instructor from the learning process. In an initial learning relationship the instructor provides a tremendous amount of guidance to the participant. The participant will be watched closely to ensure that he or she is conducting all items in accordance with the procedure. As the participant's skill grows, the instructor offers less direction to the participant.

File Transfer Protocol — A communications protocol used to transmit files without loss of data. A file transfer protocol can handle all types of files including binary files and ASCII text files. (www.techweb.com)

Firewall — A method for keeping a network secure. It can be implemented in a single router that filters out unwanted packets, or it may use a combination of technologies in routers and hosts. Firewalls are widely used to give users access to the Internet in a secure fashion as well as to separate a company's public Web server from its internal network. They are also used to keep internal network segments secure. For example, a research or accounting subnet might be vulnerable to snooping from within. (www.techweb.com)

Functional Requirements Specification — A technical document used to describe all of the requirements for a new application to be developed. It outlines system interrelationships, hardware requirements, infrastructure requirements, user requirements, and any other requirements necessary to ensure that a system will meet an organization's standards for new software and/or applications. This is one of the key documents required when identifying a potential vendor or using IT personnel to get an application developed. See sample in the Resource section of this book.

Horizontal Loading — Organizational development term that signifies what happens when an individual is given many more responsibilities and tasks, but stays at the same level or in the same job description.

Hybrid Learning Opportunity — A learning opportunity that uses a combination of traditional learning methods, e.g., classroom and alternative learning methods such as a high-tech learning solution (e.g., CD ROM or web-based learning tool).

Hyper Text Markup Language (HTML) — The document format used on the World Wide Web. Web pages are built with HTML tags, or codes, embedded in the text. HTML defines the page layout, fonts, and graphic elements as well as the hypertext links to other documents on the Web. Each link contains the Uniform Resource Locator (URL), or address, of a Web page residing on the same server or any server worldwide, hence "World Wide" Web. (www.techweb.com)

Intentional Learning — Learning that takes place in a structured learning environment that is anticipated. For instance, when a person goes to a first-year Spanish class, it is expected that the person will learn some of the basics of the Spanish language. The *intent* of Spanish class is to learn to speak Spanish.

Knowledge Management System — Systems that capture, store, and organize the experiences of workers and work groups and make the information available to others in the organization. One other key role that knowledge management systems are now playing is that of making connections. Knowledge management systems are now being used in some organizations to connect a subject matter expert(s) with the person who has a question. Organizations are often so large and have so much "churn" that knowing who to call is as important as knowing the answer.

Learning Bytes — Small chunks or bits of knowledge. Learning bytes can be reassembled into larger custom learning opportunities.

Mindshare — Getting and maintaining the attention of your target audience.

Multilearning — Learning a multitude of knowledge and skills simultaneously.

Plug-in — An auxiliary program that works with a major software package to enhance its capability. For example, plug-ins are widely used in image editing programs such as Photoshop to add a filter for some special effect. Plug-ins are added to Web browsers such as Netscape to enable them to support new types of content (audio, video, etc.). The term is widely used for software, but could also be used to refer to a plug-in module for hardware. (www.techweb.com)

PPTP — Point-to-Point Tunneling Protocol — A protocol that encapsulates other protocols for transmission over an Internet Protocol network. Due to its method of encryption, PPTP is also used to create a private network within the public Internet. Remote users can access their corporate networks via any Internet Service Provider (ISP) that supports PPTP on its servers. (www.techweb.com)

Prefigured Work — "Work that has been defined and designed in advance, for execution under a set of well-defined standard conditions. Prefigured work is usually defined and designed by someone other than the person who will be expected to accomplish it" (Nickols). *See also Configured Work.*

Synchronous Learning — In online learning, an event in which all of the participants are online at the same time and communicating with one another. For example, an instructor might schedule a guest lecturer to take questions at a particular time; all interested people would connect with the lecture when the guest is online (Carliner, p. 111). Contrast with *Asynchronous Learning*.

Uniform Resource Locator (URL) — This term is what is used to describe the location of web sites. It is normally in the www.url.domain format, where www designates world wide web, the URL is a specific name or address (for example learn2now), and the domain designates the type of site (.com for business, .edu for universities and schools, .org for organizations, etc.).

Unintentional Learning — Unexpected learning that occurs while engaged in a nonstructured learning activity.

Bibliography

"Academy" *Encyclopedia Britannica Online*
http://search.eb.com/bol/topic?idxref=407255&pm=1> Accessed April 23, 1999.

Carliner, Saul. (1999) *An Overview of Online Learning*. Amherst, MA: HRD Press.

Cohen, Norman. (1999) *The Manager's Pocket Guide to Effective Mentoring*. Amherst, MA: HRD Press.

Fahden, Allen. (1993) *Innovation On-Demand*. Minneapolis, MN: The Illiterati.

Fisher, Sharon G. (1997) *The Manager's Pocket Guide to Performance Management*. Amherst, MA: HRD Press.

Fitzwater, Terry L. (1998) *The Manager's Pocket Guide to Documenting Employee Performance*. Amherst, MA: HRD Press.

Fitzwater, Terry L. (1999) *The Manager's Pocket Guide to Employee Relations*. Amherst, MA: HRD Press.

Galbraith, Michael W. (1990) *Adult Learning Methods*. Malabar, FL: Krieger Publishing Company.

Gates, Bill. (1999) *Business @ the Speed of Thought*. New York, NY: Warner Books, Inc.

Gleick, James. (1999) *Faster*. New York, NY: Pantheon Books.

Gottlieb, Agnes Hooper, Gottlieb, Henry, Bowers, Barbara, and Bowers, Brent. (1998) *1,000 Years, 1000 People*. New York, NY: Kodansha America, Inc.

167

Haines, Stephen G. (1998) *The Manager's Pocket Guide to Systems Thinking & Learning*. Amherst, MA: HRD Press.

Hall, Brandon. (1997) *Web-Based Training Cookbook*. New York, NY: Wiley Computer Publishing.

Hiam, Alexander. (1998) *The Manager's Pocket Guide to Creativity*. Amherst, MA: HRD Press.

Imperato, Gina. (1999) "Learning without Limits." *Fast Company Magazine*, page 46.

Ishinomori, Shotaro, and Duus, Peter. (1988) *Japan, Inc.: An Introduction to Japanese Economics (The Comic Book)*. University of California Press.

Kaye, Steve. (1998) *The Manager's Pocket Guide to Effective Meetings*. Amherst, MA: HRD Press.

Marklein, Mary Beth. (April 27, 1999) "Upstart College Makes the Grade and a Profit." *USA Today*.

Meister, Jeanne C. (1998) *Corporate Universities*. New York, NY: McGraw-Hill.

Nickols, Fred. *The Autonomous Performer: Implications for Performance Technology*. 1997.

Pope, Sara. (1998) *The Manager's Pocket Guide to Team Sponsorship*. Amherst, MA: HRD Press.

Roberts, J. M. (1997) *The Penguin History of the World*. London: Penguin Books Ltd.

Schank, Roger. (1997) *Virtual Learning*. New York, NY: McGraw-Hill.

Spencer, Lyle M., and Spencer, Signe M. (1993) *Competence at Work*. New York: John Wiley & Sons, Inc.

Stark, Peter Barron, and Flaherty, Jane. (1999) *The Manager's Pocket Guide to Leadership Skills*. Amherst, MA: HRD Press.

Winslow, Charles D., and Bramer, William L. (1994) *FutureWork*. New York, NY: The Free Press.

www.techweb.com/encyclopedia.

Learning Bytes

- The American Sign Language (ASL) sign for learning is to place the dominant hand into the open, upturned palm of the other hand and quickly pull it up onto the forehead.

- Watch children in a pre-school or kindergarten at play if you want to see some examples of on-demand learning. Watch how each object or toy is picked up, tasted, pulled, tugged, licked, twisted, thrown, sat on, etc., until its secrets are uncovered.

- Tax time is a national period of on-demand learning (and mourning, I guess). The federal government and the Internal Revenue Service (IRS) change the rules every year, so we all get to "figure out" what we owe anew each year.

- When is the last time you went to class to learn a new skill outside of the work environment? If it has been greater than a month, does that mean that you haven't improved yourself in any way?

- Does your learning solution have to be in place for the ages? If not, don't build it for the ages. It can really change the way you design learning solutions in a positive way.

- The most innovative learning solution you can build or buy is useless without the complementary learning need. Don't force fit solutions to nonexistent problems. If a television set fell into the hands of some people 300 years ago, it wouldn't have been an innovation, it would have been something to display plates on.

- Is your learning accessible? Can people get to it when they want to? Or do people have to access it on some predetermined nonflexible schedule? How would you feel if a child of yours was put on a six-week waiting list to be seen for a bout of pneumonia?

- Can people get just the skill and/or knowledge they need from your learning solution? Or do they have to experience four days of theory before they can safely learn what they need to do?

- Does everyone learn the same way? No. So, it's a good idea to offer several flavors of a learning solution so that each person's learning preference is addressed. Alternatively, incorporate several learning methods in each solution so that it is cross-functional.

About the Author

Darin Hartley has been working in the training industry for the past eleven years and has undergraduate and graduate degrees in Corporate Training and Training Management. He is the Program Manager of the Dell Learning Technology Services Department of Dell Computer Corporation's training organization, Dell Learning. Darin has presented previously at ISPI International, ASTD International, and the ASTD Technical Skills Training Conference on a variety of topics. He has authored articles for *Technical & Skills Training* and *WorkForce* magazines. Darin wrote his first book, *Job Analysis at the Speed of Reality*, for HRD Press in 1999.

Prior to Dell, Darin has worked for Lockheed Martin, EG&G, General Physics Corporation, and the U.S. Navy as a nuclear power plant operator (eight years). He currently resides in Pflugerville, Texas.

Darin can be reached via email at dhartley@texas.net.